MALI

PROFILES • NATIONS OF CONTEMPORARY AFRICA
Larry W. Bowman, Series Editor

MALI

A Search for Direction

Pascal James Imperato

Westview Press
BOULDER AND SAN FRANCISCO

Dartmouth
LONDON

For my children:
Alison, Gavin, and Austin

Profiles/Nations of Contemporary Africa

Published in 1989 in the United States of America by Westview Press, Inc., 5500 Central Avenue, Boulder, Colorado 80301

Published in Great Britain in 1989 by Dartmouth, Gower Publishing Company Limited, Gower House, Croft Road, Aldershot, Hampshire GU11 3HR

Library of Congress Cataloging-in-Publication Data
Imperato, Pascal James.
  Mali: a search for direction / Pascal James Imperato.
    p. cm.—(Profiles. Nations of contemporary Africa)
  Bibliography: p.
  Includes index.
  ISBN 0-8133-0341-9
  1. Mali. I. Title. II. Series.
DT551.22.I46   1989
966.23—dc20   89-32849
                                                                               CIP

British Library Cataloguing in Publication Data
Imperato, Pascal James
  Mali: a search for direction—(Profiles: nations of
  contemporary Africa)
  1. Mali. Social conditions 1960–
  I. Title II. Series
966'.2305
ISBN 1-85521-049-5

Printed and bound in the United States of America

∞   The paper used in this publication meets the requirements of the American National
    Standard for Permanence of Paper for Printed Library Materials Z39.48-1984.

10   9   8   7   6   5   4   3   2   1

Contents

Tables and Illustrations

Preface

This work is based on twenty-three years of research, field work, and contacts with both Malians and non-Malians familiar with the country. I first began studying about Mali in early 1966 when, as a young physician in the United States Public Health Service, I was assigned to carry out a smallpox eradication and measles control program in the country funded by the United States Agency for International Development. I arrived in Mali in late 1966 and lived and worked there for five years until late 1971. During that time, I worked with twenty-four mobile health teams and visited every district in the country. Traveling with Malian colleagues by truck and canoe, on horses and camels, on foot, and by air, it was my good fortune to see Mali's great diversity and to learn much about the country while trying to alleviate human suffering. During those five years, I traveled 50,000 miles by truck alone, was sheltered in villages and nomad camps, and was the recipient of both generous hospitality and patient teaching. The friendships that I forged with Malians during those years have already entered their third decade. Since then I have made several return field visits of a few months' duration, have been in regular contact with both Malians and non-Malians familiar with events in the country, and have sent several students to do fieldwork in Mali.

This book is by no means an exhaustive treatment of Mali, and no doubt some readers will miss something of particular interest to them. However, the references cited in the notes and the selected bibliography should provide sufficient additional resources of information and satisfy both specialists and general readers.

My knowledge of Mali has been greatly enriched over the years by a large number of Malians, Americans, and nationals of other countries, and I want to thank all of them. In the preparation of this book, I was especially helped by Robert Baker of the United States Information Agency, an old Mali hand, who supplied me with much useful current information, and by the U.S. ambassador to Mali, Robert M. Pringle, who graciously arranged for me to meet President Moussa Traoré and several Malian government ministers in Washington, D.C., in October 1988.

I want to thank Lois Hahn, whose Save the Children Federation daughter, Saran Koné, lives in Kolondieba, Mali, for her careful preparation of several versions of the typescript. Larry W. Bowman of the University of Connecticut, the series editor, made many useful suggestions for improving the book, and for these I am very grateful. Special thanks are extended to Marian Safran, Jeanne Campbell, and Sally Furgeson at Westview Press for their valuable assistance in preparing this volume for publication. Thanks are given to the Longman Group Ltd. for permission to reproduce the three historical maps from *History of West Africa*, Volume 1, edited by J.F.A. Ajayi and M. Crowder, London, 1971 and 1976; to *West Africa* for permission to reproduce a photograph of President Moussa Traoré; and to the U.S. Department of State for permission to reproduce the general map of Mali. I am deeply grateful to my wife, Eleanor, and my three children, Alison, Gavin, and Austin, for their support and understanding.

Pascal James Imperato
Manhasset, New York

MALI

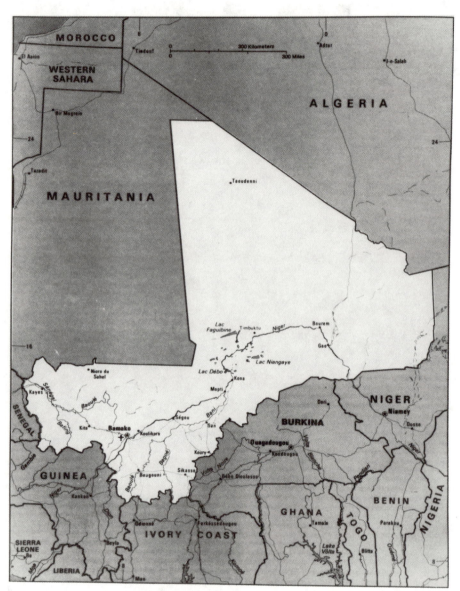

Mali (reprinted from Background Notes series, U.S. Department of State Publication 8056)

1

Introduction

Mali is a landlocked country in the semiarid interior of West Africa. Its gross national product for most of the 1980s was U.S. $1.0 billion annually, translating into $140 per capita. This makes Mali one of the poorest countries in the world. A primarily agricultural country (most of whose population depends on farming, fishing, and herding), it had an annual operating budget of $135 million during the late 1980s. By comparison, New York City had an annual operating budget of close to $20 billion during the same period. Mali's annual operating deficit during the 1980s averaged $35 million, most of it covered by external aid, especially from France. Life expectancy is currently forty-five years, with one out of every two children dying before the age of five. Because of high fertility and a high birthrate, the population is projected to reach twelve million by the year 2000 and thirty-seven million by the year 2035 if present rates of increase continue. There is little hope that the country's resources will increase, even modestly.

These basic statistics portray a bleak picture and a long struggle against enormous odds. They also tell us that human suffering, which is not easily measured and weighed, is a dominant factor in Malian life. Dependent on subsistence agriculture, the country is vulnerable to cyclical droughts and famine, two of which have occurred in the past twenty years.

The cradle of three great empires, Ghana, Mali, and Songhay, and of numerous kingdoms, Mali is the heir to many rich cultural traditions. Although many Malians continue to practice indigenous religions, Islam has made steady progress to the point where the majority of people are Moslem. This has inevitably drawn the country closer to the Moslem world.

As the French Sudan, Mali achieved independence in 1960 under the leadership of Modibo Keita, whose Marxist political views led to the creation of a state-run economy. Keita distanced Mali from France, the former colonial power, and established close political and economic

1

relations with the Eastern bloc, particularly the Soviet Union and China. Mali's worsening trade and budget deficits eventually forced Keita to reestablish a special economic and political relationship with France. However, before this was brought to full fruition, he was removed in a military coup d'état led by Lt. Moussa Traoré.

The military continued Keita's economic policies, which resulted in a bloated bureacracy and a growth in the number of inefficient parastatals, which operated at great losses. During the mid-1980s, external donors, including the World Bank, the International Monetary Fund, and France, exerted pressure on Traoré's government to modify its state-run economy as a condition for future aid. In response, Mali initiated a program of economic reform aimed at expanding the private sector and reducing the number and size of parastatals. As part of this program, the Traoré government has tried to attract European and U.S. investors. However, dismantling the huge state bureaucracy and parastatals has proven politically difficult.

Although Mali was directly ruled by the military from 1978 to 1979, civilian participation in government through a military-sponsored political party has been significant since 1979. This party, the Union Démocratique du Peuple Malien (UDPM), is organized along Marxist-Leninist lines and borrows heavily from Keita's "democratic centralism." Despite the existence of elections, a political party, and civilians in high government office, the military, under President Traoré, who as a general is head of the armed forces, still controls the levers of power.

Since independence, Malians have forged strong ties with the Communist bloc through shared political views, trade, and the thousands of men and women who have pursued advanced study in Communist countries. However, guided by President Traoré's political and economic pragmatism, Mali steadily moved closer to the West during the 1980s. Despite this recent change in direction, the country's strong socialist traditions, Marxist political and economic structures, the absence of a strong capitalist tradition, and the paucity of resources constitute major disincentives for Western investors. Mali's struggle to balance its socialist traditions and institutions with the drive to create a significant private sector in the economy will figure prominently in the political agenda for the 1990s.

MALI AND ITS NEIGHBORS

The Republic of Mali covers 478,767 square miles (1,240,000 square kilometers).[1] Shaped like an hourglass, Mali shares common borders with seven other countries, Algeria in the north, Guinea and Ivory Coast in the south, Burkina Faso and Niger in the east, and Mauritania and Senegal in the west. Mali's modern borders are a result of seventy years of French colonial rule (1890–1960). During this time, the borders were considerably modified and the name of the colony changed as well. These name changes included Soudan Français (French Sudan) (1890–1899), Sénégambie et Niger (Senegambia and Niger) (1902–1904), Haut-Sénégal et Niger (Upper Senegal and Niger) (1904–1920), and again Soudan Français (French Sudan) (1920–1959).

TOPOGRAPHY

Mali is a flat country, consisting largely of plains and plateaus. This flat relief is accented in a few places by hills and mountains. Southern Mali contains hills that are an extension of the Futa Djallon highlands of Guinea to the west. The highest peak in this region is Mount Mina, which rises to 1,739 feet. The Manding Mountains extend from the area of the Guinea-Mali border to 50 miles east of Bamako, Mali's capital, which lies on the Niger River. These mountains, ranging in height from 1,000 to 1,500 feet, consist of Pre-Cambrian rocks covered with eroded sandstone.[3] Although most of eastern Mali is flat, it contains some remarkable topographic formations. Among these are the Bandiagara Cliffs and Plateau. The former are eroded sandstone escarpments that run for 150 miles from the southwest to the northeast and reach a height of 1,200 feet.[4] To the east of the Bandiagara Cliffs are the Hombori Mountains, which are isolated sandstone mesas, some of which rise above 3,000 feet. The most important of these are the Hand of Fatima; Hombori Tondo (3,773 feet), the highest point in Mali; and Gandamia, a large stone mountain situated between the villages of Douentza and Hombori.[5]

In eastern Mali, tall riverine sand dunes, laterite hills, and rocky outcrops are found along the banks of the Niger River. The Adrar des Iforas Mountains are located in the northeastern part of the country in the *cercle* (administrative district) of Kidal. These mountains, which are part of the Hoggar Mountain system of the Sahara, consist of an ancient basement complex of sandstone rocks that have been uplifted to a height of 1,100 feet. The western portion of Mali is also hilly and accented by the Tambaoura escarpment, which consists of eroded sandstone.

One of the most important topographic features of Mali is the Inland Delta of the Niger.[6] This is a 40,000 square mile area in the center of the country, consisting of flood plains and meanders of the Niger River. These plains are flooded from June through October of each year, during and following the rainy season. The retreating waters create pasture for the livestock herds of the Peul nomads and damp areas suitable for the cultivation of cereal crops. The inland delta is the remnant of what was once a large inland lake that existed during a more rainy period. The upper Niger once flowed into this lake, whose waters joined those of the Tilemsi River draining the Adrar des Iforas Mountains in the northeast. The Tilemsi Valley and the Adrar des Iforas are now arid.

Northern Mali lies within the Sahara Desert. The topography here is variable, consisting of ergs (shifting sands), vast sandy plains in the very north known as the Tanezrouft, sand dunes, and salt pans such as those around Taoudeni, which have been mined since the sixteenth century.

RIVER SYSTEMS

Mali is traversed by two major rivers, the Senegal and the Niger, and their tributaries. Were it not for these rivers, most of what is now Mali could not support sizable human populations. The Senegal River arises in western Mali from two principal affluents, the Bafing and the Bakoye, which meet at the small town of Bafoulabe. The river flows in a northwesterly direction for 560 miles into neighboring Senegal and Mauritania, and then into the Atlantic Ocean. Enroute, it receives several other affluents. The course of the Senegal is broken by the Gouina Falls and the Felou Falls, the latter being near the town of Kayes. The river rises between July and October and falls to its lowest levels between April and May. The navigability of the Senegal River has been greatly affected by the Manantali Dam, on the Bafing River, completed in late 1988.[7]

The Niger River arises in the highlands of Guinea and Sierra Leone and then flows through Mali in a northeasterly direction. Its flow, and hence its navigability, are impeded by the Sotuba cataracts, a few miles to the east of Bamako. Several miles beyond the cataracts, the river flows through a broad, flat valley and into the inland delta beyond the town of Ségou. At Mopti, it receives its principal affluent, the Bani River, which in turn is fed by the Baulé, Bagoé, and Banifing rivers, which drain southern Mali. The Sankarani River, which in part forms the border between Mali and Guinea, flows into the upper Niger to the southwest of Bamako.

The Niger continues its northeasterly course and eventually breaks up into two principal channels, the Bara Issa and the Issa Ber. A number of seasonal lakes are found around these two branches, the most important being Debo, Fati, Teli, Tanda, Niangaye, Do, Faguibine, and Korientzé. Above Dire, the two channels join and the river flows past Kabara, the port of Timbuctoo. At this point, the river's flow becomes more easterly than northeasterly until it reaches Bourem, where it makes a great bend

The Niger River, Mali's lifeline (photo by author)

towards the southeast. It then flows past Gao, Mali's most important easterly town, and after passing over a series of cataracts it moves into the Niger Republic. The Niger River traverses Mali for 1,010 miles, nearly a third of the river's total length.

The river crests at different points along its course in response to the rhythm of the rainy season (June–October). The upper river crests in August, in the inland delta in September, and in the area of the bend in December. The river is navigable for large boats during the high water periods, August to January, from Koulikoro, just east of Bamako, to Gao.

CLIMATE

Mali possesses three climatic zones. In the south, the Sudanic climate zone extends up to 15° north latitude. It receives from 20 to 60 inches of rain per year, the lighter amounts in the northern part of the zone. North of the Sudanic zone is the Sahel (from the Arabic *sahil*, "shore"). This zone roughly extends 300 miles south to north to about 20° north latitude. In this zone, temperatures vary from 80° F in the south to 105° F in the north, and rainfall from 20 inches in the south to 7 inches in the north. The Sahara lies to the north of the Sahel, and there rainfall is sporadic and scanty, with temperatures ranging from 120° F to 140° F.

In all three zones, the climate is generally hot and dry except during the rainy season. The dry season, from November to June, is characterized by steadily rising temperatures that peak between April and June. This heat is determined in part by the harmattan, a steady flow of hot, dry air out of the Sahara, which dominates the climate from February through June. Temperatures in the Sudanic zone and the Sahel can rise to an average of 105° F during this period. From November through January, a cool air mass flows from the northeast. Known as the *alize*, it causes a brief cool spell, during which temperatures can drop to 70° F.

The monsoon winds that blow from the southwest beginning in June bring considerable moisture and usher in the rainy season, which is fairly cool and slightly humid. Most rain falls during July and August, but in the south of Mali the rains begin in May and continue through early October. Rainfall often occurs only three or four times a week, and frequently at night. The beginning and the end of the rainy season are often characterized by violent thunderstorms and gales. The latter are especially severe in the Inland Delta of the Niger. Once the rains end in October, the climate becomes warm and humid until the *alize* brings in cool air again in November.

DROUGHT AND FAMINE

Several droughts have periodically occurred in Mali, the most recent ones being in 1970–1974 and 1984–1985.[8] The 1970–1974 drought primarily affected the Sahelian zone of the country, whereas the 1984–1985 one touched most of the country, including the fertile southern agricultural regions.[9] Both droughts affected all of the countries of the Sahel, and the one in 1970–1974 attracted a great deal of media attention in the West because of the resulting severe famine. Multilateral and bilateral aid was given to Sahelian countries like Mali during most of the 1970s in order to rehabilitate them and to prevent another disaster. Yet all of this assistance—money, development projects, and technical training for Malians—did not prevent the 1984–1985 drought and its effects. The reasons for this are complex and have little to do with climate, which governments cannot control. However, governments can act to prevent the principal effect of drought, namely, famine. Still, famine initially occurred during the 1984–1985 drought.

Among the external factors causing famine were declining terms of trade in the 1970s because of stagnant economies in the industrialized countries, a fall in world prices for Malian export commodities, and an almost fivefold increase in the price of oil during the 1970s. These factors, particularly the cost of fuel, forced Mali to spend increasing amounts of its hard-currency reserves on necessities, leaving little for development projects to improve agricultural productivity.

In addition to external factors, a number of internal ones contributed to the famines that occurred during the two droughts. Prominent among these are rural-urban migrations, which decreased the number of farmers, high population growth rates, which adversely affected the country's ability to feed itself, and government agricultural policies, which kept producer prices down for food products in order to provide food at low cost to urban dwellers, who have more political clout than farmers. The government's agricultural marketing board's actions gave little incentive to farmers to increase output by expanding acreage under cultivation. In addition, peasant farmers have been largely outside of the development process and have not benefited from technological advances, which can increase the productivity of the land.

At independence, Mali was self-sufficient in food production. This situation has since markedly deteriorated and when exacerbated by droughts, has resulted in famine. Massive foreign assistance has enabled Mali to cope with its famines. But the country's ability to do so on its own in the future will require technological inputs to improve agricultural productivity, restructuring of the marketing of agricultural products so as to provide farmers with financial incentives, and a national family-planning program to limit population growth. During the 1980s, Mali greatly modified its agricultural marketing policies. This alone, however, will be insufficient to guarantee that famine will not occur again. Drought is a recurring feature in Mali; thus a broad range of interventions will be needed to deal with the factors responsible for famine.

VEGETATION AND FAUNA

The greatest variety of vegetation in Mali lies in the southern Sudanic vegetation zone. This area of the country is covered with wooded riverine forest galleries and wooded savannas. The commonest trees in this region are the shea butter tree (*Butyrosperum parkii*), caicedra tree (*Khaya senegalensis*), and silk cotton tree (*Ceiba pentandra*). Mango trees (*Mangifera indica*) were introduced into western Mali by early French administrators and have been planted around villages even as far east as Mopti. Vegetation in the Sahel is sparse, consisting of trees such as the baobab (*Adansonia digitata*), doum palm (*Hyphaene thebaica*), acacia thorn (*Acacia albida*), and cram-cram grass. As one moves northward in the Sahel, small acacia and mimosa species dominate, often interspersed with stretches of sand. The protection of the country's forests has been a concern since colonial times and a focus of more recent development aid. The major threats to forests are bushfires—purposely set by both farmers and herdsmen—overgrazing by livestock, particularly goats, and cutting for firewood by ever-expanding human populations.[10]

There was once a great deal of wildlife in what is now Mali. Large wild mammals have generally disappeared from most areas of the country due to the pressures of shifting patterns of agriculture, human population

pressure, and poaching by both Africans and Europeans.[11] Small pockets
of wildlife remain in a few areas. However, these too are under pressure.
Lions are present in small numbers in the Niger Bend, on the Bandiagara
Plateau, and in western Mali around the Faleme River, in the *cercle* of
Douentza, and around the Bani River in the *cercle* of Dioila. Until the
late 1960s, giraffes were numerous along the left bank of the Niger in
the *cercles* of Bourem, Gao, and Ansongo. However, successive droughts
greatly reduced their numbers, and by 1987 only two known specimens
were present in the wild.[12] Roan antelope are present in several areas,
as are other antelopes. Hippopotamuses are found in both the Niger
and the Bani rivers and are especially common in the Niger near
Labezanga, close to the border with the Niger Republic. Numerous
species of birds are especially common around the shallow lakes of the
Inland Delta of the Niger. Ostriches were once common, especially in
the Niger Bend, but there, too, their numbers have been progressively
reduced by the theft of their eggs by local artisans who decorate them
with multicolored leather for sale to tourists. There are two national
game reserves in Mali, the Parc National de la Boucle du Baoule in the
west, and the Menaka Reserve in the east. The Baoule covers 200 square
miles and is situated 120 miles to the northwest of Bamako. The Menaka
Reserve covers 10,000 square miles and is situated in the easternmost
part of the country.

POPULATION

Mali's mid-1989 population is estimated to be 9 million, 90 percent
of whom live in rural areas. Overall, the country is sparsely inhabited,
with densities ranging from 70 per square mile in the central areas, to
fewer than 5 per square mile in the north. The capital, Bamako, which
had a population of 320,000 in 1972, doubled in size to 600,000 in
1986, and by mid-1989 had approximately 700,000 people. Only a few
other towns have sizable populations. These include Ségou (70,000),
Mopti (60,000), Kayes (60,000), Sikasso (50,000), and San (25,000). For
the most part, urban growth outside of Bamako has been determined
by the development of local industries. The growth of the town of Mopti
is restricted by the fact that it is situated on three islands in the flood
plain and cannot expand. However, the town of Sévaré, nine miles away,
on the edge of the flood plain, has greatly expanded in recent years
because of Mopti's inability to do so.

The birthrate in Mali at present is 55 per 1,000 persons, and the
mortality rate is 32 per 1,000. The annual population increase has been
on the order of 2.5 percent for the past two decades. Sixty percent of
the population is less than twenty years of age. Life expectancy is forty-

five years, with most deaths occurring in children under two. It is projected that Mali's population will reach 37 million by the year 2,035 if present rates of increase continue.[13]

Mali's continuing population growth against the backdrop of a stagnant economy and no growth in agricultural productivity is cause for concern, as it will inevitably lead to serious economic and political consequences. The rural exodus to Bamako continues as many seek better incomes than those provided by farming. Many such migrants, however, swell the ranks of the unemployed and underemployed and place demands on the government for services that cannot be provided.

Cultural attitudes favoring a large number of offspring have blocked the initiation of significant family-planning programs in Mali. There are a number of determinants, among which are the idea that a country's importance is directly related to the size of its population and the view prevalent among many high government officials that Mali is under-populated relative to its land mass and thus capable of supporting many more people. This view ignores the idea that ideal population levels should be defined in terms of a country's resources. Islamic leaders in Mali incorrectly invoke Islam as promoting large families, providing a religious basis for what is in effect a cultural preference. Malian society is male dominated, and a man's status is relative to the number of children, especially sons, he has. Polygamy, still widely practiced, helps to ensure a man's ability to father large numbers of children.

In rural areas, it is in the parents' interests to have many children, who can assume responsibility in the family's labor-intensive subsistence farming. In the cash economy of the capital, children become a drain on a family's resources, as fees must be paid for schooling and costs incurred for food and clothing. In that setting, children do not contribute to the family's income. The government has so far not thrown its weight behind family-planning programs, although it has permitted small ones to function in Bamako and other towns. The impact of these programs on Mali's population growth has been minimal.

The population of Mali consists of several large and small ethnic groups, some of which share common linguistic and cultural charac-teristics.[14] The largest group is the Bambara (Bamana), who live in the central part of the country along the middle Niger and its affluents. They number close to 3 million at present. The Malinke (Maninka), who are closely related to the Bambara both linguistically and culturally, number 500,000 and live in the south and southwest of the country. The Peul (Fula), who number 800,000, live in and around the Inland Delta of the Niger. Unlike the Bambara and the Malinke, who are primarily agriculturists, the Peul are herdsmen. The Sarakole (Soninke), the heirs to the ancient Ghana Empire, live in the northwest in the

Peul woman winnowing millet, Kona (photo by author)

Sahel and number 600,000. Many of them are farmers, but others are traders known for their worldwide trading networks. Over the past several decades, large numbers of Sarakole have migrated to France. The Songhay, who number 500,000 and live along the Niger Bend, are riverine cultivators of cereal crops and to a lesser extent livestock owners. The Dogon, well known for their remarkable representational art and their religious beliefs, made famous by the French anthropologist Marcel Griaule, number 400,000 and live in and around the Bandiagara Plateau and Cliffs. They are subsistence farmers. The Senufo and Minianka live in southern and southeastern Mali, number 500,000, and are subsistence farmers. Northeast of them live the Bobo, who are also farmers and who number 200,000. Along the Niger live the Bozo and Somono fishermen, who together number around 50,000. In addition to these groups, there are several smaller ones, including the Tuareg nomads of the northeast, who number 50,000, the Maure nomads of the Sahel, who number around 60,000, the Diawara (80,000), Khassonke (15,000), Tukulor (5,000), and Dioula (10,000). The Maure and Tuareg are pastoralists, whereas the others are subsistence farmers. In addition to being farmers, the Dioula are also traders. In the central, western, and southern parts of Mali, Bambara is the lingua franca. In the Inland Delta of the Niger, Fulfulde, the language of the Peul, is the lingua franca, and in the northeast Songhay is widely spoken. Bambara tends to be spoken in most administrative centers because a high proportion of administrators are Bambara.

The Bambara and Malinke dominate the political life of the country for several reasons, including their geographic proximity to the seat of national government, Bamako, and because they embraced education early in the colonial period. They were thus able to move into positions as teachers and government functionaries and from there to organize political parties.

Ethnic rivalries and ethnicity have not been major features of the Malian political scene to date. The various ethnic groups in the country often complement one another economically, as for example the Bambara farmers, Peul herdsmen, and Bozo fishermen do. The diverse farming groups such as the Bambara, Dogon, Malinke, and Songhay do not compete for the same lands and do not produce sufficient surplus to become marketplace rivals.

The national political system has easily accommodated all ethnic groups, whose representatives have often looked after their constituents' interests. Advantages provided to all groups and not at the expense of others have served to keep most satisfied. As Mali's population grows and its urban centers increase in size, these long-standing harmonious ethnic relations are apt to break down. There are already early signs of this: Ethnic preferences in hiring are exercised in some state-owned and private enterprises; such preferences in the allocation of building lots in Bamako and admission to school also occur. In the emerging urban cash economy, ethnic diversity may lead to conflict in a world of limited resources. Eventually, this could move into the political sphere, leading to divisive ethnic politics. Interethnic marriages are frowned on by most families, and within specific ethnic groups marriage is restricted to the members of one's own caste.

The one unifying cultural element in Mali that transcends ethnicity is Islam. Approximately 65 percent of Mali's population count themselves as Moslems, and the remainder follow indigenous religions. Among many professed Moslems, elements of indigenous religions are often retained. There are in Mali several different Moslem brotherhoods, primarily distinguished by variations in ritual observances and practices. In general, these brotherhoods do not have organizational control over followers, and their leaders exert little political influence.

There are some 80,000 Catholics and Protestants in Mali. Most are in the capital and in the *cercles* of Tominian, San, and Bandiagara. Social and economic pressures often have forced a number of Christian Malians to convert to Islam.

Tuareg couple, Hombori (photo by author)

The Malian government is keenly aware of the potential dangers of sectarian politics and has frequently reaffirmed that the state is laic in character. Nevertheless, most political leaders are Moslem, and this, coupled with the adherence of most of the population to Islam, has led to special relationships with the Arab and Moslem worlds.

2

Early History

Archaeological studies have uncovered traces of human activity going back several millennia in what is now Mali. The oldest human remains were found at Asselar in northern Mali in 1927 by Theodore Monod and others.[1] In the early 1970s these remains were dated by carbon 14 to 4400 B.C. Neolithic settlements have been documented in diverse areas of the country, including Nioro, Gao, Bamako, and Bougouni. In addition, prehistoric rock paintings and engravings have been found in many areas, especially in the northern part of the country. Those in the north indicate that several millennia B.C. the Sahara was well watered by rivers and lakes and possessed abundant wildlife, including elephants, giraffes, rhinoceroses, and aquatic animals. The Sahara progressively underwent desiccation, and by 500 B.C. it had assumed its present shape and characteristics. Rock paintings in the central Sahara range in age from 6000 B.C. to 100 B.C. and trace the environmental changes that occurred and human responses to them. Horse-drawn chariots appear around 1200 B.C., whereas camels are not depicted until 100 B.C., reflecting the more arid climate.[2]

Sometime around the end of the second millennium B.C., populations in this area changed from hunting and gathering and began to cultivate cereal crops.[3] Copper was in wide use in the Western Sudan as early as 500 B.C., and a few hundred years later ironworking was introduced.[4] The use of these metals by certain groups gave them military superiority over those who did not possess them. The twelfth-century geographer Al-Zuhri recorded that the armies of Ghana possessed swords and spears and attacked their neighbors, who fought with only ebony sticks.[5]

Recent archaeological excavations in Mali's Inland Delta of the Niger at Djénné-Jeno (Jénné-Jeno) have uncovered evidence that an ancient town existed at the site as early as the third century B.C.[6] The results of these excavations, carried out between 1977 and the present, have greatly modified previous theories about urban development in sub-Saharan West Africa. It appears that Djénné-Jeno was continuously

15

occupied between 250 B.C. and A.D. 1000. Between A.D. 300 and A.D. 800, large burial urns were used and luxury goods were abundant, indicating sophistication and success in trade. After A.D. 800, mud bricks were used in house construction and terra cotta statues made for ritual purposes.[7] The former discovery altered the belief derived from Islamic sources that mud brick construction was introduced into what is now Mali by the Andalusian architect, Ibrahim es Saheli (died [d.] 1346), who returned from Mecca with the Mali emperor, Kankan Moussa, in 1325. It is thought that Djénné-Jeno may have had a population of 10,000 by A.D. 800, when it reached its zenith.[8] Thereafter the town appears to have gone into decline. Based on currently available information, the nearby town of Djénné was not founded until the thirteenth century.

GHANA

The Arab conquest of North Africa eventually brought both Islam and trade across the Sahara to the peoples of what is now Mali. Both were to have a major impact in shaping society south of the Sahara. The initial focus of contact for traders from North Africa was the kingdom of Wagadu, situated in what is now northwestern Mali. Information about Wagadu, which the Arabs called Ghana, has come to us from three principal sources, the writings of Arab geographers and chroniclers, local oral traditions, and archaeological studies. The evidence recorded by Arab geographers of the time and Arab writers of later centuries varies greatly, perhaps representing changing perspectives of the kingdom over time. Oral traditions recorded in the twentieth century provide yet differing accounts. However, through all of these accounts runs the common thread that the kingdom of Wagadu, or Ghana, was intimately involved in the gold trade.[9]

Ghana, founded by the Soninke, who are the northernmost Mande peoples, may have arisen as early as the fourth century A.D. The name *Ghana* appeared in written Arabic sources in the 830s; it was associated with gold. The first detailed account of Ghana was given by the Arab geographer El Bekri in 1067/8. He described the city of Ghana as consisting of two towns: one royal, where the king lived, and the other several miles away, where the Moslem traders lived. El Bekri also provided detailed accounts of the king's court and the system of taxes on imported goods.[10] Ghana imported luxury goods from North Africa, along with copper and salt, and exported gold. The control of the gold fields in the southwest was essential to Ghana's political hegemony and economic prosperity.

The borders of Ghana must have regularly been in a state of flux, and those to the north seem to have been determined by the balance of power between the kingdom and the Sanhaja nomads, who lived in the desert. It appears from El Bekri's account that Ghana reached its zenith in the middle of the eleventh century. Ghana's decline came about shortly after that, principally as a result of the Almoravid invasion of sub-Saharan West Africa. The Almoravids installed a Moslem as king of Ghana; most previous kings had been animists. However, Ghana was then little more than a small kingdom surrounded by a number of small successor states that had risen in prominence in the wake of its collapse. One of the most important of these was Sosso, which lay to the southeast of Ghana. It emerged into a powerful Soninke state in the twelfth century and came into open conflict with the emerging kingdom of Mali in the early thirteenth century. Sosso invaded Ghana and in so doing brought about Ghana's complete decline. Another important successor state was Diafunu, which arose in the western regions of the former Ghana kingdom. Mema, situated southwest of Timbuctoo in the northern Inland Delta of the Niger, was also a successor state, founded, according to some traditions, by the chief of the king's slaves of Wagadu (Ghana). Some claim that Mema was the closest political and religious heir of the Ghana kingdom.[11]

The French ethnographer and colonial administrator Maurice Delafosse was the first to suggest that the stone ruins at Kumbi-Saleh, in southern Mauritania near the border of Mali, may have been those of the capital of ancient Ghana. Excavations carried out at the site on several occasions have revealed the remains of a town built of stone and measuring a mile square.[12] It is estimated that the town had as many as 15,000 inhabitants. These ruins may represent the Moslem merchant quarter of the old city of Ghana. The royal town, built as it was of biodegradable materials, has vanished with little trace. Whether these ruins represent the capital of the Soninke kingdom is still an open question.

Ghana was successful as a political state in the Western Sudan for several reasons. It was headed by powerful rulers who exercised strong central authority, extended its influence over the neighboring areas, and effectively controlled the gold trade. The kings remained animist, adhering to an ancestral religion that gave them, in the eyes of their subjects, a supernatural quality, which the kings used to political advantage. Yet, Moslems who were literate were not excluded either from trade or from the administration. This acceptance of Islam and Moslem traders ensured the continued economic well-being of the state because the traders were essential to the trans-Saharan gold commerce.

Ghana was distinguished as a national state from its successors, Mali and Songhay, in that it consisted of a single ethnic group, the Soninke. Although its influence did at times extend beyond Soninke frontiers, it was essentially homogeneous in ethnic terms. Mali and Songhay, in contrast, came to rule over large numbers of alien peoples who regularly revolted when power at the center weakened.

THE ALMORAVID INVASION

The Almoravids were Islamic reformers who, through proselytization and military conquest, brought the western Sahel, Sahara, Maghreb, and the Iberian Peninsula under their control. The Almoravid movement arose among the Sanhaja of the western Sahara in the early part of the eleventh century. Eventually, the group split in two with Abu Bakr Ibn 'Umar becoming head of the southern faction, which controlled vast areas of the Sahara and the Sahel. Abu Bakr launched a series of wars against Ghana and its allies over a fourteen-year period extending from 1062 to 1076. The disruption of trade, which resulted from the wars, was a severe blow to a kingdom whose power depended on commerce. As a consequence, Ghana was subject to significant attrition and finally total conquest. The Almoravids converted many of the Soninke to Islam and installed a Moslem as king of Ghana. Many of the non-Moslem Soninke fled, joining their brothers on the fringes of the ancient Ghana kingdom, where they found refuge in small successor states. Internal divisions among Abu Bakr's followers contributed to a decline of his power, and in 1087 he was killed in the Sahara near Tagant while trying to suppress a revolt.[13]

MALI

Ghana no longer existed at the beginning of the thirteenth century. Its hegemony over vast areas of the western Sudan was to be assumed by Mali, which had its beginnings as a small Malinke kingdom around the upper reaches of the Niger River. Information about the Mali kingdom, or empire, as it is sometimes called, comes from local oral traditions, external Arabic sources, and the writings of sixteenth- and seventeenth-century scholars in Timbuctoo.[14] The early history of Mali is unclear. However, around A.D. 1230, Soundiata Keita (also known as Mari Djata), the son of a Malinke chief of the Keita clan, became the head of Mali, then a small vassal state of Sosso. Ibn Khaldun (1331–1382), an Arab historian residing in North Africa, provided some of the most detailed information about Soundiata and Mali, which he obtained from travelers and traders who had been to Mali.

The Sankore Mosque, Timbuctoo (photo by author)

Soundiata, who in Malinke traditions is a god-hero, consolidated his power over the Malinke chiefs through his leadership in the struggle to free them all from the rule of Sosso, then led by Soumangourou Kanté.[15] In Malinke oral traditions, Soumangourou is portrayed as an antihero figure and a sorcerer. In a fight in 1235 between the armed forces of Sosso and Mali, at Kirina, near modern-day Koulikoro, Soumangourou was defeated. This victory for Soundiata transformed Mali from an alliance of independent Malinke chiefs into an empire. Soundiata continued his conquests and by 1240 had established Mali's hegemony over most of what is now western Mali and portions of Senegal and Guinea. Mali already controlled the Boure gold fields in the south, and its conquest of Sosso gave it access to the trans-Saharan trade routes.

Following the death of Soundiata, the leaders of Mali were referred to as *mansa* (king). Soundiata's son and successor, Mansa Uli, made a pilgrimage to Mecca during the reign of the Mamluk sultan of Egypt, Baybaro (1260–1277). Mansa Uli's pilgrimage provides confirmation that Islam was the court religion and documentation for the dates of rule of a Mali king. Succession to the throne within the Keita clan briefly ended when Sakoura, a former court slave, usurped power. He became one of Mali's most powerful rulers, expanded its territory, and made a pilgrimage to Mecca during the reign of the Egyptian Sultan El Malek (1298–1308).

Sakoura was killed on the Horn of Africa on his return, and the throne reverted to the Keita clan again.

Around 1317, Mansa Moussa (also known as Kankan Moussa) became king, and in 1324–1325 he made a pilgrimage to Mecca. Although Mansa Moussa was not a prominent figure in oral traditions, his pilgrimage put Mali on the map in both figurative and cartographic terms. His arrival in Cairo in 1324 was the most significant event of the year. His generous gifts and expenditure of gold caused the value of gold in Cairo to plummet. Because of his pilgrimage, "Rex Melly" appears on the 1339 map of Angelo Dulcert and "Musa Melli" on the famous Catalan map drawn in 1375 for the Emperor Charles V by Abraham Cresques of Majorca. Under Mansa Moussa, who also initiated diplomatic relations with the sultan of Morocco, Mali reached its peak of territorial expansion (see Map 2.1).

Following Mansa Moussa's death around 1337, various Keita clan members contested succession to the throne, which led to civil war and coups d'état.[16] It was during this period that Ibn Batuta (1304–1378), a Moroccan traveler and geographer often called the Marco Polo of Islam, visited Mali. Ibn Batuta began his two-year trip to the Western Sudan in 1352 and reached Niani, the capital of Mali. There he was received by the Mali ruler Souleyman (c.1341–1360). His firsthand descriptions of Mali's social, economic, and political life and his descriptions of other areas of sub-Saharan West Africa are a major historical source for this area of Africa.[17]

The sociopolitical infrastructure of Mali consisted of an elaborate kinship system composed of lineages and clans, organized on territorial lines into villages and districts. As in most early states in the Western Sudan, noble clans defined the empire's political history, exerted authority over other societal groups such as freemen, serfs, and slaves, and ultimately over other non-Malinke peoples. Slaves were the backbone of ancient Mali, as well as of Ghana, Songhay, and other early states in the Western Sudan. They cultivated lands for local chiefs, who used the products to support their own administrative apparatus and their armies and to send tribute to the imperial center. Slaves also served as bowmen in the army and were frequently chosen for important administrative posts because their lack of clan and family allegiances meant that they could be trusted. They also played an important political role at the imperial center in Mali.

The king's role in maintaining the strength and integrity of the state was a crucial one. The history of Mali makes it clear that the empire prospered under strong and wise rulers and began to weaken under inept ones. Slaves and counselors usually came to the rescue

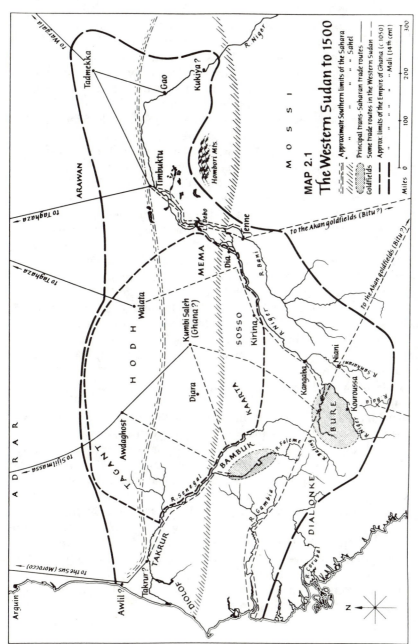

MAP 2.1
The Western Sudan to 1500

Approximate Southern limits of the Sahara
" " " Sahel
Principal trans-Saharan trade routes
Some trade routes in the Western Sudan
Goldfields
Approx. limits of the Empire of Ghana (c 1050)
" " " Mali (14th cent)

Miles 0   100   200   300

Map by Neil Hyslop. Reprinted, by permission, from *History of West Africa*, J.F.A. Ajayi and Michael Crowder, eds., vol. 1, p. 117. © 1971, 1976 Longman Group Ltd.

when the ruling dynasty faltered, either by usurping the throne for themselves or on behalf of a better qualified prince.

A number of inept rulers followed Souleyman, and succession to the throne was frequently contested, passing between usurpers and various branches of the Keita clan. This instability at the center provided incentive for rebellion in the outlying provinces. By the late fourteenth century the Malinke center of the empire was unable to protect trade and provide security in the Sahelian periphery, where Mali ruled over conquered alien peoples. However, Mali retained control at the Malinke center and in the west. With Ibn Khaldun's death in the late fourteenth century, the continuous record of what transpired in Mali ended. Portuguese traders recorded in the fifteenth century that the inhabitants of Gambia were still the subjects of the ruler of Mali, and there were sporadic contacts between Mali and the Portuguese colonists on the coast in the late fifteenth and early sixteenth centuries.

Leo Africanus (1493–1560?), an Arab born in Fez, went to the Western Sudan in 1510 with his uncle, who was sent as an emissary to Songhay by the sherif of Fez. Leo Africanus visited Djénné and Mali and described Mali's domains as extending west to the Futa Djallon, south into the forest, and east to Djénné.[18] Es Sadi (1596–1655), a scholar born in Timbuctoo, documented the rise of the Bambara state of Ségou in the eastern domains once ruled by Mali and Mali's failed attempt to conquer the Bambara between 1667 and 1670.[19] Thereafter, Mali broke up into small independent chiefdoms, and the Keitas retreated to Kangaba, where they became provincial chiefs.

At its peak in the fourteenth century, Mali extended from Senegal and Gambia in the west to Gao in the east and from what is now southern Mali to Walata in the Sahara. The Keita dynasty of Mali was unique in the early states of the Western Sudan in that it ruled for four centuries. In other states, even founding dynasties were overthrown. This staying power reflects both the prestige of the Keita dynasty and the almost religious respect with which it was held. For in spite of disputes at court, usurpations, and the eventual erosion of the empire's periphery, the dynasty survived and continued to rule a Malinke homeland. Mali's principal weakness was that it was a heterogeneous empire in which difficulties at the imperial center opened the way for revolts at the periphery. The weakening at the center was frequently rectified by strong rulers or powerful usurpers who quickly retrieved lost provinces. Mali's retreat from the eastern Sahel opened the way for the emergence of Songhay hegemony in this area.

SONGHAY

The Songhay Empire began as a small chiefdom along the banks of the Niger River in present-day eastern Mali. The impetus for its growth and that of its capital, Gao, was the salt trade that originated in the Taghaza mines in the Sahara and the gold trade, over which Songhay assumed control after Mali's decline. According to some traditions, the rulers of Songhay converted to Islam in the early eleventh century. Songhay was then a vassal state of Mali, and in 1324 and 1325 Kankan Moussa, the Mali ruler, visited Gao and received the homage of Za Yassiboi, the Songhay ruler. Two of Za Yassiboi's sons traveled to Mali with Kankan Moussa. One of them, Ali Kolon, escaped and returned to Songhay, where he eventually succeeded his father as ruler around 1335. He took the name Sonni (meaning savior) and established a lineage that lasted until 1492. There were a total of twenty Sonni kings, the most eminent of whom was the next to last, Sonni Ali Ber (d.1492), who ruled from 1465 to 1492. A warrior-king, he greatly expanded Songhay, conquered Timbuctoo, annexed parts of Mali, and eventually made Songhay independent of the latter.[20]

His son and successor was quickly overthrown by a Soninke, Mohammed Touré, who had been a lieutenant in Sonni Ali Ber's service. Touré took the title Askia and became known as Askia Mohammed or Askia the Great. The Za dynasty that Askia Mohammed replaced had ruled Songhay for almost six centuries. His own dynasty of elven Askias would rule for slightly less than one hundred years. Mohammed made the pilgrimage to Mecca in 1496. Later, he launched a number of jihads (holy wars) against both Moslem and non-Moslem states and expanded the frontiers of his empire westward to the headwaters of the Senegal and eastward into what is now Niger and Nigeria[21] (see Map 2.2).

In 1529, Askia Mohammed was overthrown by his son Moussa. The empire reached its zenith under Askia Daoud (1549–1583), who was another son of Askia Mohammed. Three of Daoud's brothers and one of his cousins had reigned before him, often forestalling coups and eliminating rivals. In contrast, Daoud's relatively long reign of thirty-four years was peaceful. The *Tarikh-el-Fettach*, a historical work, and the Timbuctoo scholars made much of Daoud's piety and Islamic virtues.

Daoud was succeeded by four of his sons in what were to be the last nine years of Songhay as a state. Upon Daoud's death in 1583, one of his younger sons, Askia El Hadj Mohammed, usurped power. He had the rightful heir, Mohammed Bankanu, imprisoned and then successfully defended himself against the attempts of yet another brother, Kurmina Fari el Hadi, to dethrone him. In 1586, a third brother, Mohammed Bani, overthrew El Hadj Mohammed and had the two imprisoned rival brothers executed. This act of fratricide exacerbated the dynastic struggle.

Songhay, by this time, had gained control of the gold trade that moved toward North Africa through urban entrepôts (intermediate trading centers) such as Djénné and Timbuctoo. The Moroccan ruler, el Mansur,

24

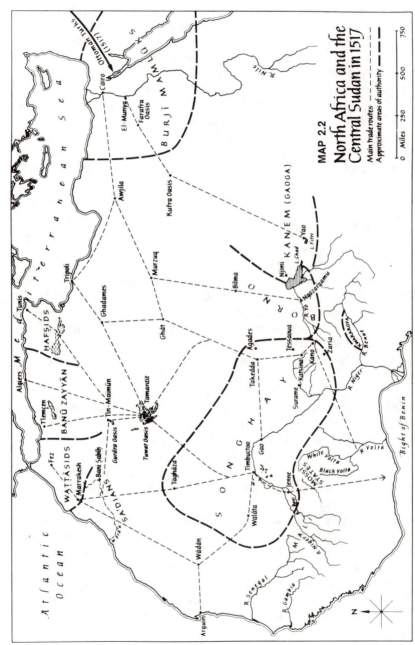

MAP 2.2
North Africa and the
Central Sudan in 1517

Main trade routes ----
Approximate areas of authority ▬ ▬

0   250   500   750
Miles

Map by Neil Hyslop. Reprinted, by permission, from *History of West Africa*, J.F.A. Ajayi and Michael Crowder, eds., vol. 1, p. 226. © 1971, 1976 Longman Group Ltd.

had designs on both the salt trade and the gold of Songhay. In 1585, the Moroccans seized the salt mines at Taghaza, and Songhay responded by opening mines at Taoudeni.

In 1588, another son of Askia Daoud, Mohammed el Sidiq, who commanded the western military garrisons headquartered in Timbuctoo, rebelled. The merchants of Timbuctoo, chafing at the taxes levied on them by the Askia, supported el Sidiq, as did the Maghsharen Tuaregs, who had suffered great economic losses because of the Moroccan seizure of the Taghaza salt mines. El Sidiq was proclaimed Askia in Timbuctoo by his supporters. Askia Mohammed Bani set out from Gao to subdue him but died en route. On April 18, 1588, Askia Ishaq II, another son of Askia Daoud, was proclaimed Askia in Gao. He marched against el Sidiq, defeated him, and executed the chief of the Maghsharen Tuareg. This was a tactical error for Ishaq because the Maghsharen Tuareg were a superb mounted military force that would have been indispensable in repelling the Moroccans, who invaded three years later (see Map 2.3).

The constant fratricidal struggles among Askia Daoud's sons greatly weakened Songhay as a military power. Split by rivalries and grudges over past wrongs, the various power factions were unable to put their differences aside and unite behind the Askia Ishaq II, who faced an invasion that was eventually to destroy Songhay.[22]

THE MOROCCAN INVASION

Ahmed el Mansur became sultan of Morocco in 1578 and aspired to be the universal caliphate (the leading ruler in Islam). His expansionist policy included the conquest of Songhay, which he viewed as the source of immense quantities of gold. He was not aware of the fact that gold arrived in North Africa from Songhay's leading entrepôt, Timbuctoo, after passing through middlemen and traversing domains not fully controlled by Songhay. El Mansur began harassing Songhay during the reign of Askia Daoud by taxing the salt leaving Taghaza and annexing the oases of Touat and Gurara, which were essential to the trans-Saharan trade. Moroccan control of Touat provided el Mansur with an ideal location from which to spy on Songhay.

The wars in Songhay between the sons of Askia Daoud did not go unnoticed by el Mansur, who by 1589 decided that the time was ripe to invade. In October 1590, el Mansur mustered an army of 4,000 soldiers and 600 support staff and turned them over to a young commander, Djouder, a Spaniard from Las Cuevas. Many of Djouder's soldiers were European captives well trained in the art of warfare with muskets. Djouder's invasion force included 10,000 camels, 1,000 pack

26

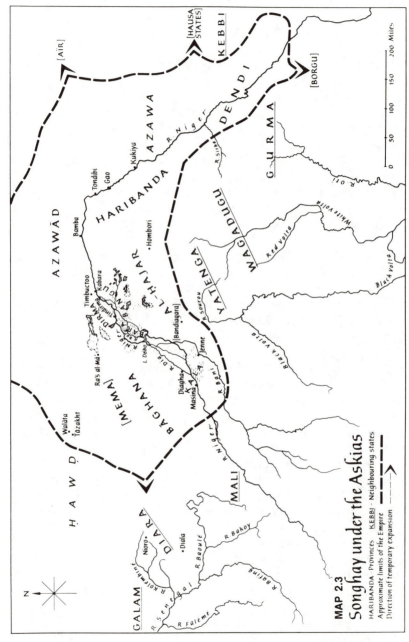

MAP 2.3
Songhay under the Askias
HARIBANDA - Provinces   KEBBI - Neighbouring states
Approximate limits of the Empire ————
Direction of temporary expansion – – – – ➤

Map by Neil Hyslop. Reprinted, by permission, from *History of West Africa*, J.F.A. Ajayi and Michael Crowder, eds., vol. 1, p. 291. © 1971, 1976 Longman Group Ltd.

horses, muskets, gunpowder, and 10 mortars that fired stone balls. Djouder entered the Sahara in late December and within two months was on the banks of the Niger River in the heart of Songhay.

Askia Ishaq II was aware of the Djouder's descent toward Songhay but could do nothing to stop him until Djouder was near the river. The recent civil wars in Songhay had resulted in the death of many of the kingdom's best soldiers, and consequently Ishaq's army consisted of many unseasoned recruits. Askia Ishaq assembled an army of about 40,000 men, equipped with spears and bows and arrows. The two armies finally clashed at Tankondibo near Tondibi, 35 miles north of Gao. The Songhay panicked when faced with muskets for the first time and fled south to Gao. This brief but decisive battle resulted in very few casualties on either side. Ishaq, fleeing to the other side of the river, tried to negotiate with Djouder, offering to recognize Moroccan supremacy and pay an annual tribute to el Mansur. Djouder was inclined to accept the offer because his position and that of his men was precarious. He communicated Ishaq's offer to el Mansur, and then he moved his army to Timbuctoo after spending seventeen days in Gao. Ishaq had suggested the move in the hopes that once in Timbuctoo, Djouder would withdraw.[23]

The Moroccan occupation of Timbuctoo was at first greeted warmly. However, the boorish behavior of Djouder's men and Djouder's seizure of housing for his army and imposition of taxes led to open conflict with the religious scholars and merchants of the city. El Mansur was enraged when he received Djouder's letter and the preliminary tribute sent by Ishaq; el Mansur's response was to send a replacement to Timbuctoo, Mahmoud bin Zergoun, who arrived in August 1591. Zergoun's orders were to destroy the Songhay army, and with that in mind he and Djouder engaged the Songhay again, this time east of Timbuctoo near Bamba. The Songhay were routed, and the defeat roused them to depose Ishaq and replace him with his brother Askia Nouh early the next year. Military engagements between Nouh and the Moroccans continued for two more years, but these came to nothing. The Songhay retreated to Dendi in the southeast, where they continued to rule a small state for a while. Djénné was occupied by the Moroccans.

The Moroccans, however, never dominated more than the central stretch of the Niger River. Beyond it, a state of anarchy developed in the void left by the removal of Songhay power and influence. Smaller states eventually emerged to fill the void, but for many years trade was severely disrupted because of the absence of security in so much of the Western Sudan. The period of Moroccan domination is referred to as the Pashalik because pashas originally governed in the name of the sultan. They ruled from Timbuctoo, the early ones having been sent out from Morocco—the last of these arriving in 1604—whereas the later ones were locally elected. Effective Moroccan influence ended seventy years after the invasion, by which time the descendants of the invaders governed their own affairs. There was a great deal of troop replacement in the early years of the occupation, and, in fact, the original invading army eventually returned to Morocco, being replaced by Berbers in 1599.

The Moroccan soldiery was known as Ruma, which was locally transformed to Arma, a group that still lives in the region of the Niger Bend of modern Mali. The military strength on which the Moroccans based their rule gradually waned. In part, this was due to internecine struggles among the invaders, who elected and deposed pashas with great frequency. Incessant wars with adjacent small states and the Tuareg, whose power was in ascendancy, eventually reduced Ruma power to that stretch of the Niger between Timbuctoo and Gao. The Tuareg achieved a major victory over the Ruma in 1737 at Toya, and thereafter they were the masters of the Niger Bend. The Ruma retreated to Timbuctoo, where they continued to be a powerful force for another century. The title *pasha* disappeared in 1775, reemerged twenty years later, and persisted until 1833 when the Peul defeated the Ruma at Dire.[24]

TIMBUCTOO AND DJÉNNÉ

The cities of Timbuctoo and Djénné figure prominently in the early history of Mali because they were centers of scholarship and the principal commercial entrepôts through which most of the trade passed after the fall of Ghana. Timbuctoo was founded as a seasonal camp for the Tuareg nomads in the eleventh century. The Mali ruler, Kankan Moussa, passed through it in 1325 on his return from Mecca and, according to local traditions, had the mosque known as Dyingerey Ber built by his Andalusian architect, Ibrahim es Saheli. Timbuctoo increased in importance as trade shifted from the old trans-Saharan routes used in the days of Ghana to the east. In 1468, the city fell to Sonni Ali Ber, the ruler of Songhay, who because of his animist beliefs was not always on cordial terms with the city's religious scholars. Under Askia Mohammed (1492–1529), Timbuctoo flowered both intellectually and commercially, in part because of the Askia's respect for Islamic scholarship, which he encouraged, and in part because of the security provided by his armies. The Moroccan invasion of 1591 effectively destroyed Timbuctoo's intellectual life.[25]

Timbuctoo had gained a reputation in the Islamic world because of the writings of a number of its scholars. Among these was Ahmad Baba, who was a member of the Aqit family of the city. He wrote many books and treatises, a number of which have survived to this day in

Egypt and Morocco. One of his most important works was *Nayl al-Ibthikāj*, which was widely read in North Africa.

The religious scholars of Timbuctoo, collectively known as the *ulama*, participated in ruling the city, which during the time of Songhay was a city-state within a state. These men were members of powerful trading families, which gave them access to a network of patronage and power. The Moroccans viewed the *ulama* as a potentially dangerous group. In 1593, the literati of Timbuctoo were instrumental in launching a revolt against the Moroccans, and in retaliation some of them were killed, others imprisoned, and yet others exiled to Morocco. Their private libraries were confiscated, and according to local accounts, Ahmad Baba alone lost 1,600 books. He and some other scholars were sent in exile across the Sahara to Marrakesh, where they were imprisoned until 1595. Their release was facilitated by the intervention of Moroccan Islamic scholars, many of whom had been opposed to el Mansur's invasion of a neighboring Moslem state. Ahmad Baba did not return to Timbuctoo until 1607/8, but while in Morocco extensively wrote and taught. He died in Timbuctoo approximately twenty years after his return.[26]

Timbuctoo also had many other notable scholars, among whom was Mohammed Kati (1468–?), a judge during the reign of Askia Mohammed. A number of Western scholars have credited him with writing the *Tarikh-el-Fettach*. However, in recent years, others have challenged this view.[27] Es Sadi (1596–1655) was a later scholar who became the imam in Djénné and who is credited with authorship of an important historical work, the *Tarikh-es-Sudan*. The presence of a large number of scholars in Timbuctoo created a demand for Islamic texts, and not surprisingly, one of the major imports into the western Sudan during the time of the Songhay kingdom was books.

Timbuctoo's economic base was trade, with merchandise entering it from North Africa and from the hinterland of the Western Sudan. During the time of Songhay, its principal imports were European cloth, sugar, brass vessels, horses, and books. Its principal exports were gold, slaves, and civet, which was used in the manufacture of perfumes. Addax skins, out of which the Moroccans made shields, were also exported.[28] Salt came into Timbuctoo from the mines at Taoudeni, which were under the control of Songhay.

The Moroccan invasion of 1591 sent Timbuctoo's commercial life into steep decline. The once-flourishing trans-Saharan trade was greatly diminished by the early eighteenth century, due in part to a shift of slaves and gold to the new European trading stations that had been established on the coast. Timbuctoo successively fell under the rule of numerous groups, including the Bambara, Tuareg, Peul, and finally the French, who occupied it in 1894. Today, Timbuctoo is a small town of

15,000, primarily built of gray mud brick. Salt still comes down to the town from the mines at Taoudeni, but now it arrives primarily by truck.

Djénné's history is closely linked with that of Timbuctoo. A city situated on an island in the lower reaches of the Inland Delta of the Niger and noted for its distinctive mud brick architecture, it was founded in the fourteenth century near the site of Djénné-Jeno, which has been discussed earlier in this chapter. First under the control of Mali, it was captured by Sonni Ali Ber of Songhay in 1468 and later fell to the Moroccans. Much of the merchandise that moved in and out of Timbuctoo passed through Djénné. Djénné played a major role as an entrepôt for the salt that was brought in from Taoudeni, 438 miles north of Timbuctoo. From Djénné, the salt was traded into the interior, where it was at a premium.[29] In the early nineteenth century, Djénné fell under the rule of Cheikou Amadou Bari, was occupied by the Tukulor under El Hadj Omar Tall in 1862, and finally annexed by the French in 1893.

THE RISE OF OTHER KINGDOMS

The fall of Songhay and the inability of the Ruma to successfully provide economic and political stability over the geographic area of the former Songhay empire, opened the way for the development of new states. To their credit, the Ruma did master the art of political stability but were unable to extend their influence beyond a limited stretch of the middle Niger. Thus, during the period of the sixteenth through nineteenth centuries, important kingdoms developed in the area of the middle Niger. The Bambara kingdom of Ségou emerged in the early seventeenth century under the leadership of Biton (Mamari) Coulibaly (c.1712–1755). He greatly expanded the borders of what had been a powerful chiefdom, transforming it into an ethnically cohesive state through the use of a standing army, the *ton djon*. Both of Coulibaly's sons and heirs, Dikoro and Ali, were eventually deposed by the *ton djon*, and in 1766 the army made N'Golo Diarra king (*fama*). His descendants ruled Ségou until 1862, when the kingdom was invaded by the Tukulor under El Hadj Omar Tall.[30] The Tukulor were never able to fully subjugate the Bambara, who remained in control of vast areas to the south and east of Ségou.

The Diarra dynasty under Ali Diarra was temporarily reinstated in Ségou in 1890 by the French Gen. Louis Archinard after the Tukulor had been driven out. However, Ali Diarra was later removed and executed by the French resident Captain Underberg for plotting the assassination of French officers.

Also in the seventeenth century, another Bambara kingdom emerged to the northwest of Ségou and was ruled by the Massassi Bambara.

Known as Kaarta, it did not achieve the military strength nor the degree of political power enjoyed by Ségou. It was not until the nineteenth century that Kaarta developed into a significant political state. It was quickly destroyed in 1854 by El Hadj Omar Tall and the Tukulor.

To the east of Ségou, a Peul kingdom emerged in the flood plains of the Niger as early as the fifteenth century. Founded by Maga Diallo, this kingdom was originally a vassal state of Mali. Called the Peul kingdom of Macina (the name of a pond near Tenenkou) by modern scholars, it became a powerful force in the inland delta after the fall of Songhay. Eventually, Macina became a vassal state of the Bambara kingdom of Ségou. Maga Diallo's descendants ruled this state until 1810, when they were ousted by a Moslem cleric, Cheikou Amadou Bari (1755–1844), who ushered in a period of militant Islamic revival that was to dominate the Western Sudan for most of the nineteenth century.

Cheikou Amadou had traveled to northern Nigeria, where he became a disciple of Osman Don Fodio, a religious leader who had established a theocratic state there. On returning to Macina, Amadou preached against the ruling Peul dynasty and their Bambara overlords. A charismatic leader, he attracted many followers and in 1810 defeated a combined force of Peul and Bambara. Establishing his capital at Hamdallaye, near present-day Mopti, he set up a theocratic state (*dina*) and was subsequently succeeded by his son Amadou Cheikou in 1844, followed by his grandson Amadou Amadou, in 1852. All three took the title Amirou al Moumenina (commander of the faithful). The Peul Empire of Macina became a well-developed political state during the fifty years of its existence. Cheikou Amadou promulgated a broad range of laws, freed Macina from Bambara domination, and subjugated Timbuctoo. He also destroyed the great mosque at Djénné, in part because its beauty offended his fundamentalist beliefs.[31]

In 1862, El Hadj Omar Tall, the Tukulor jihadist, attacked Macina and had Amadou Amadou executed. The fall of Macina was facilitated by dynastic jealousies on the part of two of Amadou Amadou's senior cousins, Ba Lobbo and Abdul Salam. They withheld their full military support for Amadou Amadou, hoping that a Tukulor victory would put him aside and leave them as leaders of the *dina*.

In southern Mali a small kingdom, Kénédougou, was founded by the Dioula in the seventeenth century. The most important leader of Kénédougou was Tieba Traoré (1845–1893), who became king in 1877. Tieba was a skilled military tactician and an adroit diplomat who greatly expanded Kénédougou's domains. In 1887, he was attacked in his new capital, Sikasso, by Samory Touré, a Dioula imam warrior. The siege lasted fifteen months and was broken by the arrival of a French military force. Tieba, in return for being rescued from Samory, signed a treaty with the French giving them a protectorate over Kénédougou. He died in 1893 and was succeeded by his brother Babemba, who expanded the kingdom's borders into present-day Burkina Faso and Ivory Coast. In 1898, Babemba repudiated the arrangement with the French by refusing to send an annual tax of eighty head of cattle and by expelling from Sikasso the French military ambassador. By this time, the French were fully in control of most of what is now Mali. Using Babemba's defiance as an excuse for military action, they attacked Sikasso on April 15, 1898, and took the city on May 1, whereupon Babemba committed suicide.

A number of small states emerged in what is now western Mali. These included Khasso, Logo, Gajaga, and Diarra. Gajaga and Diarra were successor states to Ghana and lasted into the nineteenth century, often as vassal states of their more powerful neighbors. Khasso and Logo assumed importance in the midnineteenth century because the former, under the leadership of Dyoukou Sambala, allied itself with the French and the latter, led by Niamody, was a vassal of the Tukulor.

THE TUKULOR EMPIRE

El Hadj Omar Tall (1794–1864) was a Tukulor Moslem cleric whose jihad and its aftermath dominated political events in the Western Sudan for the latter half of the nineteenth century. Tall popularized the Tijaniya Sufi order of Islam throughout much of what is now Mali and directed his jihads against the established traditional nobilities of the area and the Qadiriya order espoused at the time in Macina.[32] His conquests brought Tall into direct conflict with the French, whose commercial interests his activities put in jeopardy, especially along the Senegal River. He spent five years in Mecca and seven in Sokoto (Nigeria) with Mohammed Bello, the *khalifa*, one of whose daughters he married. Originally from the Futa Toro of present-day Senegal, he eventually settled in the Futa Djallon, where he came to be respected for his wisdom and wealth, the latter obtained through trade.

In 1852, he announced that he had received a divine revelation and launched his jihad. Although the French had originally supplied Tall with arms, they ceased when it became apparent that he posed a major threat to their commercial monopolies and colonial expansion. In 1854, Tall attacked Kaarta and in 1857 blockaded Medine, a fort established by the French in what is now western Mali. Medine, which was to be crucial as a launching point for future French exploratory and military expeditions, was finally relieved by French reinforcements.

Tall had no great desire to confront the French because he had to deal with rebellions in the areas he had conquered, disloyalty among his own followers, and other campaigns. In 1861 he conquered Ségou, and the following year Macina. The Peul forces of Ba Lobbo and Abdul Salam joined with those of Sidi el Bekaye, chief of the Kounta Arabs of Timbuctoo and a leading figure in the Qadiriya Islamic brotherhood. On February 6, 1864, they attacked Tall at Hamdallaye, driving him and his forces into the Bandiagara Plateau, where he was surrounded by the Peul forces and killed.[33]

Upon Tall's death, his son Amadou, who had already been installed in Ségou, claimed succession over the entire empire. However, he was challenged by Tall's other sons and commanders, each of whom had independent armies. This led to a series of indecisive civil wars between Amadou and his rivals. Allegiance to Amadou was at best tenuous, and even within Ségou he faced rebellion among the Bambara.

Amadou Tall became head of what Western scholars have called the Ségou Tukulor Empire while his cousin, Tijani Tall, became head of Macina after finally routing the Peul.[34] Amadou's greatest threat was the French, whose movement from the west eventually culminated in General Archinard's attacking Ségou in 1890. Amadou took temporary refuge in Macina, where Tijani had died three years earlier. Pursued by the French, he eventually fled to northern Nigeria and died there in 1898.

SAMORY TOURÉ'S DOMAINS

Samory Touré (c.1830–1900) was a Moslem imam warrior who in the latter half of the nineteenth century established a large but loosely knit state across what is now southern Mali and adjacent areas of the Ivory Coast, Guinea, and Burkina Faso. Born into a Dioula merchant family, he eventually became a powerful local chief. Eventually taking the title of *almamy* (prayer leader), he launched local wars of annexation that culminated in his capture of the town of Kankan in 1879. Samory's military successes eventually came into direct conflict with the ever-advancing forces of the French. His first skirmish with the French was in 1882, and in 1883 he had another military encounter with them near Bamako. By this time, Samory had brought under his control a huge area stretching from the Niger River south to the forest and from the Tukulor domains in the east to what is now Sierra Leone in the west. Although small regions within his domains kept their autonomy, they were loosely governed from above by a central authority at his capital, Bissandougou.

Around 1884, Samory's religious fervor increased and he announced his plans of imposing Islam on the entire empire. However, he was eventually thwarted in this and his political aims by the French, who had arrived in the western Sudan in force. In 1885, he engaged the

Amadou Tall, head of the Ségou Tukulor Empire (reprinted from Abdon-Eugène Mage, *Voyage dans le Soudan Occidental*, 1868, Paris)

French at Nafadie in the present-day *cercle* of Kita in Mali and was routed. Finally, in 1887 he signed the Treaty of Bissandougou with the French by which he ceded the left bank of the Niger River to them. He then attacked Tieba of Kénédougou, who was eventually relieved by the French. Two years later, he revoked the treaty and expanded into present-day Burkina Faso, Ghana, Ivory Coast, and Sierra Leone, and he also destroyed Kong, the Dioula capital that had allied itself with the French. Samory was seen by the French as a dangerous impediment to their securing the Niger. In 1898, they made a determined effort to conquer his domains and finally captured him in the northern Ivory Coast. He was sent into exile in Gabon, where he died in 1900.[35] With his capture, his armies disbanded and his empire collapsed.

FROM THE GOLD TRADE TO ISLAMIC REVIVAL

The development of Ghana was intimately linked to the gold trade, which reached the outside world through a trans-Saharan route. Ghana was largely a monoethnic animist state whose rulers accommodated Islam and Islamic traders and administrators in the interests of larger political and economic goals. The Almoravids upset the security of the trans-Saharan trade and in so doing jeopardized Ghana's economic stability. Most scholars weighing the available evidence conclude that the Almoravid invasion of Ghana effectively destroyed it as a meaningful polity in the Western Sudan.

Unlike Ghana, Mali was a polyethnic state that emerged from a strong Malinke center. Like Ghana, its economic prosperity rested on the gold trade, which crossed the Sahara over a more easterly route via Djénné and Timbuctoo. The political strength of the state was a reflection of its rulers. Under strong rulers Mali prospered, and under weak ones it faltered. Revolt and secession of peripheral provinces threatened frequently. When the center finally weakened beyond repair, because of internecine struggles, the periphery split off into several independent states.

The more easterly Songhay state, under the aggressive leadership of the Sonni and Askia oligarchies, filled in the void left by the dissolution of Mali. Songhay, like Mali, emerged from a homogeneous ethnic cluster to extend its hegemony over heterogeneous peripheral groups. Like Mali and Ghana, its economic stability was due to the gold trade. Struggles within the Askia oligarchy greatly weakened Songhay both economically and politically just prior to the Moroccan invasion. The last years of Songhay were characterized by coups d'état and armed conflicts between rivals among the ruling class. These events are extremely well chronicled, whereas what transpired just before Mali's fall is not. It is likely that Songhay might have gone the way of Mali even without the Moroccan invasion. As it was, Songhay's immediate demise was similar to Ghana's in that Songhay was overrun by a foreign invading army.

The cities of Timbuctoo and Djénné long played important roles in the economic and political life of the western Sudan. As entrepôts for gold, salt, slaves, and other trade items, they were essential to the region's economic prosperity. Both became centers of Islamic learning, particularly Timbuctoo, whose scholar-merchants flowered under Mali and Songhay. However, the Moroccans saw these scholars as a dangerous force and either killed them or sent them into exile. Literate civilization in the western Sudan went into sharp decline with the Moroccan invasion.

The decline of Songhay and its commercial centers, Timbuctoo and Djénné, would probably have come in time due to the establishment of competing European trading posts on the West African coast. The gold and slave trade eventually shifted south out of the old Songhay heartland to closer coastal areas.

There was scarcely a pause in state building following Songhay's fall, for the Bambara of Ségou and the Peul of Macina soon developed powerful and ethnically homogeneous states. This state building took on a militant religious character with Cheikou Amadou's successful coup d'état against the ruling Diallo dynasty of Macina in 1810. He established an Islamic state that adhered to the Qadiriya brotherhood. Amadou and his successors lived in peaceful coexistence with their powerful neighbors, the Bambara. Although Islam had diffused throughout the Western Sudan with traders since the time of the Ghana empire, under Amadou it became a unifying force for state building.

El Hadj Omar Tall, the Tukulor Moslem cleric, used Islam and the jihad to carry state building forward on a grand scale throughout the western Sudan. As a follower of the Tijaniya brotherhood and as a militant, his conflict with Qadiriya Macina was almost inevitable. Tall's rapid victories over the animist Bambara and Macina between 1854 and 1867 made him the master of most of the Western Sudan. However, his unwillingness to accommodate animism and diversity in Islamic practices, specifically the Qadiriya, doomed his state, which on his death was fought over by rival heirs and commanders. Tall was unable to transform rapid military victory into a politically stable and economically prosperous occupation.

His son, Amadou, partially succeeded in achieving these ends in Ségou, an area of Tall's empire. However, he was under almost constant threat from the Bambara, whom he never fully subjugated and whose allegiance he never won. The animist Bambara, over whom the Moslem Tukulor ruled, had long tolerated Islam and had even incorporated syncretic elements into their indigenous religion. But Amadou, like his father before him, never accepted the need to maintain a balance between the interests of Islam and those of animism. The two rulers militantly and uncompromisingly promoted the interests of Islam to the detriment of those of the Bambara and were rewarded by constant rebellion and only nominal control of vast areas of the middle Niger.[36] This was a great inherent weakness of the Ségou Tukulor state, whose ruler placed his hopes on universal conversion to Islam and on Islam as a unifying force transcending ethnic boundaries. Thus, when the French finally struck their military blow, the Tukulor found themselves quite alone and without significant numbers of Bambara allies. The Bambara, for their part, were pleased to see the alien Tukulor driven from their homeland and viewed the arriving French as catalysts for reviving a Bambara kingdom.

Islamic revival in the form of state building came to an end in the Western Sudan with the French conquest of Samory Touré's domains. Although Touré's state was extensive, it lacked cohesion and the internal allegiance of heterogeneous groups whose interests frequently diverged from those of Samory. The French exploited these weaknesses and used military force in order to eliminate Samory, whom they viewed as a major obstacle to their imperial designs on the middle Niger.

3

Conquest, Colonial Rule, and Independence

Although what is now Mali was to become a French colony, the first Europeans to visit that area were British explorers. This was a reality not lost on the subsequent architects of French imperialism. They saw their dream of control of the middle Niger threatened by the historical claims and imperial expansion of Great Britain in West Africa.

EARLY EXPLORERS

Major Houghton, a British military officer, arrived in the Faleme River Valley in southwestern Mali in 1791. He explored the ancient gold fields of the Bambouk and later died at Nioro, failing to reach his goal, Timbuctoo. Mungo Park (1771–1806) was a Scottish physician who made two extensive trips through present-day Mali. His first voyage began in 1795 in the Gambia, from there traveling to the Senegal River and into the Bambara kingdom of Kaarta. After escaping from the Maures who detained him, he went on to Ségou and Sansanding but was refused an audience with the Bambara king, Monson Diarra. He returned to the Gambia via Koulikoro, Bamako, and the Faleme River, arriving on the coast in 1797. Park returned to the area in 1805, intending to sail the Niger River to the sea; he reached Bamako overland and then went on to Sansanding, where he constructed a raft. He sailed down the river but was under constant attack by various riverine peoples, including the Tuareg, who prevented him from entering Timbuctoo. Nevertheless, Park managed to navigate the Niger into what is now northern Nigeria, where he was killed at Bussa in an ambush. One of his African companions, Amadi Fatoumi, escaped from Bussa and brought back a description of Park's last days.

Between 1818 and 1821, two British military officers, Maj. William Gray and Staff Surgeon Dochard, made trips alone and together into

Bambara modes of dress in the midnineteenth century (reprinted from Abdon-Eugène Mage, *Voyage dans le Soudan Occidental,* 1868, Paris)

western Mali. Dochard got as far east as Koulikoro and was the first European to visit the Niger River since Mungo Park. In 1826, another British military officer, Maj. Gordon Laing (1794–1826), attempted to cross the desert from Tripoli in order to reach Timbuctoo. He reached Timbuctoo that year but was murdered by his Berabich Arab escort near Araoune, on the return trip.

The quest for what Europeans considered to be the "fabulous" city of Timbuctoo motivated the voyage of a Frenchman, Réné Caillié (1799–1838). Dressed as a Moslem and pretending to be an Egyptian, he started from the coast in April 1827. Nine months later, he was near San in central Mali, and in March he arrived in Djénné. From there, he traveled by boat on the Niger to Timbuctoo, arriving there on April 20, 1828. In early May, he joined a trans-Saharan caravan and finally reached Tangiers. Caillié was the first European to reach Timbuctoo, return alive, and provide a written description of the city. Jean-Baptiste Raffenel, a French naval officer, made two extensive trips into western Mali, one in 1843–1844 and the other in 1847, in the hopes of finding the source of the Nile.

Heinrich Barth (1821–1865), a German explorer working under British patronage, undertook a remarkable journey into eastern Mali, coming down from Tripoli in 1850. He traveled through what is now northern Nigeria and Cameroon, moved westward into Mali, crossed the Niger River, and made his way to Timbuctoo, arriving in 1853. He remained there under the protection of the chief of the Kunta Arabs, Sidi el Bekaye, for eight months. Barth then returned via northern Nigeria, crossed the Sahara, and reached Europe in 1855. Oskar Lenz (1848–1925) was an Austrian explorer who visited Timbuctoo in 1880, coming down from Morocco. From Timbuctoo he traveled west to Nioro and arrived at the French fort at Medine on October 18, 1880. Lenz was the first European explorer to see Timbuctoo since Barth had been there twenty-six years before.[1]

EARLY FRENCH CONQUESTS

The initial architect of French conquest of Mali was the French general, Louis Léon César Faidherbe (1818–1899). His two terms as the governor in St. Louis, Senegal, 1854–1861 and 1863–1865, were decisive for French imperial interests. Faidherbe's dream was of a French empire stretching from Senegal to the Red Sea. Although this dream was only partially fulfilled, it did result in the creation of French West Africa, which was to endure intact until 1958. Faidherbe was supported by Bordeaux-based traders who constantly lobbied for promotion of their commercial interests in West Africa. Once the slave trade was abolished, traders concentrated on gum arabic, a resin from the acacia tree, which was in high demand for fixing textile dyes and for starching clothes. French traders prodded their government into constructing a series of forts along the Senegal River to provide protection for trade. The need to protect these very parochial French commercial interests was used by Faidherbe and others as a way of rationalizing their own imperial designs.

Faidherbe's basic approach to conquest was to construct a series of forts linked by telegraph and supported by small, mobile military units. By 1855, Faidherbe had set up a fort with a military force of 1,300 at Medine in western Mali near the present-day town of Kayes. His grand design could not be implemented without direct conflict with a number of indigenous African states, and it was to take almost half a century to be realized. In order to make territorial acquisition more palatable at home, the on-site proponents of French imperialism and their supporters preferred annexation via treaty. Military operations involving loss of life were viewed as a second choice but were ultimately used with success in a series of decisive engagements.

Faidherbe and his successors sent a series of diplomatic/exploratory missions to Amadou Tall, head of the Ségou Tukulor Empire. This state was the leading indigenous power in the region and the major obstacle to French imperial designs. In 1863, Faidherbe sent Abdon-Eugène Mage

The French explorer Abdon-Eugène Mage (reprinted from Abdon-Eugène Mage, *Voyage dans le Soudan Occidental*, 1868, Paris)

(1837–1869) as an emissary to Amadou with the purpose of obtaining permission to build a string of forts as far east as Bamako and to put gunboats on the Niger River. Amadou kept Mage and his companion, Dr. Quintin, at Ségou for two years and finally signed a commercial treaty in return for the promise of arms.

French traders based in Senegal were convinced that their future prosperity in the region lay in linking trade in Senegal with that in Algeria via the Tukulor domains. With these interests in mind, the French governor of Senegal from 1876 through 1881, Col. Louis-Alexandre

Brière de l'Isle, revised Faidherbe's plans for the conquest of the Western Sudan. His addition to Faidherbe's basic plan was the construction of a railway between the navigable portions of the Senegal and Niger rivers. In 1878, he sent Paul Soleillet, a French soldier and commercial agent, to Ségou to obtain a trade agreement from Amadou Tall. Amadou was well aware of long-term French intentions and rebuffed the Soleillet mission. In addition, after the French annexation of Logo in 1878, Amadou made it known that normal relations could not be established until Brière de l'Isle was removed.

Brière de l'Isle used calculated diplomatic overtures with the Tukulor to temporize while he was trying to muster support in France for military conquest of their domains. In 1879, he sent then Capt. Joseph Simon Gallieni (1849–1916) on a diplomatic mission to Amadou Tall. En route, Gallieni signed treaties of protection with local chiefs in western Mali, thus consolidating French control. Gallieni arrived at Nango on the outskirts of Ségou in June 1880 and remained there until March 1881, during which time he tried to negotiate a treaty with Amadou Tall. The French government never ratified the Treaty of Nango, as it was called, because it promised Amadou arms; and Amadou later repudiated the treaty, claiming that his Arabic version made no mention of a French protectorate over him.

Amadou Tall's aim in his dealings with the French was to keep them at bay through diplomatic means. At no time did he intentionally confront them with military force, as did Samory Touré. The reasons for this strategy had to do with Amadou's assessment that he could not win in such a confrontation. During the early 1870s, Amadou was involved in civil wars in Kaarta with his half brothers, Abibu and Moktar, and later had to deal with a succession of rebellions among the Bambara. So much of Amadou's military resources had to be used to keep the Bambara subjugated and to forestall rebellions among his own underlings that he did not have the reserve to take on the French. The Bambara, as we have seen, saw the Tukulor as an alien oligarchy that they very much wanted to overthrow. Bambara attempts to regain independence manifested themselves in rebellions against Amadou. As it was, large segments of the Bambara country were free of Amadou's control. In the Baninko and in Beledougou, local Bambara chiefs acted as independent rulers. However, sometimes their actions unwittingly furthered Amadou's objectives. A dramatic example of this was Chief Naba Traoré's attack on Gallieni's expedition at Dio in 1880. Gallieni was traveling east to Ségou to negotiate what would be the Treaty of Nango with Amadou. The western Bambara viewed this ostensibly peaceful French gesture as a potential alliance against them and responded with military force, inflicting serious losses in life and property. Amadou, for his part, could not have been more pleased, since his intent was not an alliance but a diplomatic strategem to keep the French out.

Brière de l'Isle and other French imperialists were concerned that the British might seize the middle Niger from their footholds in either Gambia or Sierra Leone. Thus, French control of Amadou's domains was crucial. Although Brière de l'Isle was recalled in 1881, in 1880 he had set up a separate military region called Upper Senegal under a military officer with the title commandant-supérieur du Haut Fleuve. Lt. Col. Gustave Borgnis-Desbordes was appointed to the post. With headquarters at Medine, the new commander lost little time in moving eastward militarily, occupying Bamako in February 1883. Borgnis-Desbordes's military campaigns, which included encounters with Samory, aroused opposition in France because of the loss of 194 French soldiers. Opposition also arose because the railway had moved forward only 10 miles east of Kayes, and the Chinese and Moroccan laborers who were building it suffered a high mortality rate. As a consequence, in December 1883 the French parliament refused to vote for the funds necessary to continue the railway. However, this was only a minor setback for the forces of imperialism.

Also in 1883, a gunboat, the *Niger*, was transported overland from Medine to Koulikoro, where the Niger becomes navigable downstream. The following year, two naval officers, Davoust and Dellanneau, sailed it through the heart of Amadou's kingdom to Diafarabe, east of Ségou.

FINAL ANNEXATION

Final French annexation of what is now Mali was achieved primarily through the efforts of Gallieni and Louis Archinard (1850–1932). Gallieni became the commandant-supérieur in 1886. In order to forestall British incursions, he launched a series of diplomatic efforts aimed at Samory Touré and Amadou Tall. Both of the latter viewed these overtures as useful expedients to promote their self-interests. In 1887, Gallieni took military action against Mamadou Lamine Dramé, a Soninke religious cleric who, leading a movement of Soninke nationalism, had set up a state in what is now western Mali and eastern Guinea and Senegal. Dramé directed a jihad against both the French and the Tukulor, which explains why Amadou Tall allied himself with Gallieni at that time. In May 1887, Amadou signed the Treaty of Gouri, agreeing to a French protectorate and allowing French traders access to the Niger. Gallieni also sent Captain Etienne Péroz the same year to negotiate the Treaty of Bissandougou with Samory Touré. This treaty gave the French control over the lands on the left bank of the Niger and thwarted the efforts of British colonial officials in Sierra Leone, who were urging their government to declare a protectorate over Samory's domains. For his part, Samory saw the treaty as freeing him to use his full military forces against Tieba Traoré, king of Kénédougou.

During Gallieni's brief term as commandant-supérieur, the colonial imprint was put on most of western Mali. He set up *écoles des otages*, schools for the children of important local leaders, transplanting the idea from Senegal, where Faidherbe had started such a school in 1857. He also established *villages de liberté* (freedom villages) for refugees of local wars and ex-slaves. He elaborated a policy of *tache d'huile* (oil spot), in which a center of French control was expanded, using the power of local chiefs.

When Gallieni left in 1888, the railway had reached Bafoulabe. His successor was Lt. Col. Louis Archinard, who quickly initiated a series of military operations, some without the approval of his superiors.[2] It was through these military measures that much of Mali from Kayes to Bandiagara came under French control. Archinard's forces entered Ségou in 1890 and Macina and Bandiagara in 1893. Although he was dismissed in 1893 when a civilian government was appointed, he had conquered the Ségou Tukulor Empire and greatly weakened Samory Touré. Archinard was replaced by Lt. Col. Eugène Bonnier, who, contrary to the orders of the newly appointed governor of the French Sudan, Albert Grodet, launched a military expedition against Timbuctoo.

Bonnier's subordinate, Lt. Gaston Boiteaux, who was in an advance party, did not wait for Bonnier but entered Timbuctoo on his own. Bonnier arrived in Timbuctoo on January 10, 1894, almost three weeks after Boiteaux, and was dismayed to learn of Boiteaux's actions. Bonnier and Boiteaux had come by boat on the river, whereas Maj. Joseph Joffre, who would later achieve fame as a World War I general, led a land force. Bonnier marched southwest toward Goundam to rendezvous with Joffre but was killed in a Tuareg ambush on January 15. Joffre finally occupied Timbuctoo on February 12, 1894. Five years later, in 1899, Lieutenant Klobb erected forts at Gao and Ansongo in the eastern part of Mali. In 1898, Babemba, king of Kénédougou in southern Mali, was defeated, and Samory Touré was defeated and captured. It required several more years for the French to pacify the adjacent desert areas and to put down local uprisings.[3]

THE POLITICAL FAILINGS
OF THE SÉGOU TUKULOR EMPIRE

The Islamic revival states founded by El Hadj Omar Tall and Samory Touré imposed alien ruling oligarchies on ethnically heterogeneous groups in the western Sudan. These groups, which were animist for the most part, viewed their ethnic and religious interests as inextricably bound together. The militant Islamic orthodoxy of the Ségou Tukulor state was unable to accommodate Bambara ethnic and religious interests. Thus, the Bambara, who constituted the largest ethnic group in the state, felt no allegiance to the Tukulor and viewed them as both alien and inimical to their interests. The security and strength of the Ségou Tukulor state were further eroded by strong adversarial Bambara chiefdoms around the western and southern frontiers, by Bambara rebellions within the state, and by disputes and wars among the Tukulor themselves.

Historical outcomes in the Western Sudan might have paralleled the Ethiopian Emperor Menelik's success at maintaining independence in the Horn of Africa had the Tukulor been able to rally the support of the ruled through religious accommodation and political power sharing. Certainly, the cost to France in terms of lives and military expenditures would have been much greater if the Bambara had mobilized to help the Tukulor. As it was, Amadou Tall found himself without allies, and vast numbers of his subjects were only too happy to see him routed.

COLONIAL RULE

The nature of colonial rule in Mali was similar to that in other French West African territories. The colony was divided into *cercles*, or administrative units, which in turn were divided into cantons, headed by local African leaders. The canton chiefs had both judicial and tax-collecting responsibilities, recruited men for forced labor, and served as intermediaries between the administration and the population. Canton chiefs were often chosen from among the ranks of local families with a legitimate claim to traditional authority. However, individuals not belonging to traditional ruling families were sometimes appointed because of their ability to read and write French and their proven loyalty to the colonial government. Some of the unpopular duties of canton chiefs, coupled with their subordinate position in the administrative hierarchy and their reliance on the colonial government for their authority, eroded their influence and legitimacy. Many viewed them as nothing more than the agents of the French.

There were usually several cantons in a *cercle*, headed by a French commandant. The canton chiefs reported directly to the commandants, who in turn reported to the governor. Commandants had broad authority and could order the arrest and detention of Africans without trial even for petty offenses. However, this was usually imposed for nonpayment of taxes, refusing to work on labor gangs, and showing disrespect toward colonial officials. The colonial government rationalized the legitimacy of forced labor on the grounds that it was generally used for public works projects such as road building. Key administrative positions in the capital of the colony and at the *chef-lieu* (headquarters) of the *cercle* were occupied by the French. Africans largely were support personnel: clerks, typists, messengers, house servants, and interpreters.

The colonial administration of the French Sudan was highly centralized. The commandants of the *cercles* reported to the lieutenant governor (governor after 1937), who in turn reported to the governor-general of French West Africa in Dakar. The 1904 decree creating French West Africa provided for an advisory body to the lieutenant governors. In the French Sudan, this council of advisers consisted of senior civil servants, who were mostly French, and unofficial representatives chosen by the local chamber of commerce and a limited African electorate. The latter advisers included traders and provincial and canton chiefs. After 1939, military veterans and the holders of certain commercial licenses (to hold these, one had to deposit a sizable amount of money with the government) were given membership on the council.

The constitution of the French Fourth Republic, which was promulgated in October 1946, gave expanded participation in government to French overseas colonies. This constitution provided for a French Union assembly and territorial assemblies; the latter were given the power to raise and spend territorial revenues and to elect representatives (known as senators) to the Council of the Republic and counselors to the Assembly of the French Union. Under the Fourth Republic, the category of *sujet* (subject) was abolished. As subjects, most inhabitants of the French Sudan and other territories did not enjoy the rights of citizens and were subject to the *indigénat* (customary law) administered by native tribunals. The *indigénat* was frequently used by the French for tax collection, forced labor, and military conscription. Moreover, the new constitution made residents of French overseas colonies citizens of the French Union. This change in civil status was highly significant considering that in 1937 only 72,000 people in all of French West Africa were citizens.

As in other overseas colonies, the French had initially adopted a policy of "assimilation," the goal of which was to educate Africans so that they could assimilate French culture, considered superior to Islamic and indigenous cultures. Following World War I, because of the diversity and numbers of people living in the French overseas territories, the French abandoned that policy and in its place adopted one of "association." Under the new policy, African peoples and cultures, through their association with French culture, would evolve from a primitive state toward a highly civilized French ideal. Association provided a rationale for French imperialism and for practices such as forced labor, rule by decree, and the absence of elections, which were unacceptable in republican France.

The philosophy of association also provided a basis for limiting higher education in the French Sudan and other colonies. Since only a small number of assimilated Africans were needed to mediate between French culture and the masses of associated Africans, there was no need for large numbers of secondary schools. The underlying racism of both philosophies, especially that of assimilation, stimulated a counterreaction asserting African pride and culture. Léopold Sédar Senghor, the first president of Senegal, and others, were exponents of this movement, called *négritude*.

The name of the French colony as well as its borders were changed several times during the seventy years of colonial rule. On September 6, 1880, what is now western Mali was constituted as the region of the Upper Senegal and placed under a military officer. At first, Medine was the region's headquarters; the following year, the headquarters were moved to nearby Kayes, which became the colony's first capital. On August 18, 1890, the region of Upper Senegal became the French Sudan (Soudan Français) under the terms of a decree that put it under the general direction of the governor of Senegal. It was headed by the commandant-supérieur and given its own budget. On August 27, 1892, the French Sudan was given complete autonomy from Senegal and reported to the home government. The title of commandant-supérieur was then changed to that of lieutenant governor. The following year, 1893, a civilian administration replaced the military one.

On June 16, 1895, the federal government of French West Africa was formed, with the governor of Senegal as governor-general. The French Sudan lost the province of Bakel and part of Bambouk to Senegal, and Faranah to Guinea. An October 17, 1899, decree made more sweeping changes in the French Sudan. The huge territory was broken up, with large areas going to French Guinea, Dahomey, and Ivory Coast. The colony was then called Upper Senegal and Middle Niger (Haut-Sénégal et Moyen Niger), a name that would remain until 1902, when it was changed to Senegambia and Niger (Sénégambie et Niger) (1902–1904). During these periods, the eastern part of what is now Mali was administered as part of three military districts.

On October 18, 1904, French West Africa (Afrique Occidentale Française) was created as a federation of France's West African colonies. The colony's name was changed to Upper Senegal and Niger (Haut-Sénégal et Niger), a name that would be used until 1920. The three eastern military districts were incorporated into the colony, which had its own budget; a lieutenant governor was its chief administrative officer. The capital, which had been at Kayes since 1881, was transferred to

Bamako in 1908 because of its better location and because the railway from Kayes had reached it in 1904. In 1911, the military district of Niger (now the Niger Republic) was detached, and in 1919 Upper Volta was created by detaching seven districts from Upper Senegal and Niger. On December 4, 1920, a decree was issued restoring the name of French Sudan (Soudan Français). Upper Volta was abolished in 1932, with part of its territory going to the French Sudan, but finally reconstructed in 1947 and its territory returned.[4]

The title of lieutenant governor for the chief administrator of the French Sudan remained in place until 1937, when it was changed to governor. In 1959, just prior to independence, a high commissioner replaced the governor.

The colony was served by several very able lieutenant governors and governors, among whom were William Ponty (1899–1908), Jean Henri Terrasson de Fougères (1924–1931), and Edmond Jean Louveau (1946–1952). Ponty, who later became governor-general of French West Africa (1908–1915), is regarded as having been one of the most illustrious lieutenant governors of the colony. His achievements in economic and military policy were numerous. He made special efforts to stamp out indigenous slavery, created liberty villages for freed slaves, and fostered trade, development, and education. The Ecole William Ponty, the first institution of higher learning in French West Africa, was named after him in 1918.[5] Many members of the generation that was instrumental in obtaining independence from France were trained at this school.

EARLY CHALLENGES TO FRENCH RULE

Armed resistance to French colonial rule occurred during the first two decades of the twentieth century. In 1908, the Dogon ambushed and killed a French administrator and his armed escort near Dalla on the Bandiagara Plateau. This uprising was quickly put down through the use of force. In 1914, the Oulleminden Tuareg, under their chief, Firhoun Ag El Insar, revolted in the eastern part of the country. A severe drought that began in 1911 had caused much hardship and dissatisfaction among the Tuareg, who attributed their plight in part to colonial administrative policies. Firhoun was able to catalyze this dissatisfaction into a revolt at a time when the French were suffering losses in the war in Europe and reducing their military presence in the colonies. The Oulleminden revolt was quickly put down and Firhoun sentenced to ten years of imprisonment and twenty years of banishment. However, in 1916 he was pardoned and released. He and his followers rebelled again and unsuccessfully attacked Menaka, a post in the extreme east of Mali. Firhoun was killed in a final engagement with colonial troops on June 25, 1916, at Anderamboukane.[6]

In the central part of the country, two serious revolts broke out during World War I. The first was led by a Bambara chief, Koumi Diossé Traoré (1840–1915). Koumi Diossé had cooperated with the French in their assault against the Tukulor but in 1904 was exiled to Timbuctoo for refusing to provide porters. In 1915, he led a large-scale revolt of the Bambara in the Beledougou area north of Bamako, protesting conscription of his people into the army for the war in Europe. The French finally sent an expeditionary force against him and put down the revolt. Koumi Diossé and his followers committed suicide prior to the final defeat of their forces.[7] In 1916, the Bobo in the *cercle* of San revolted over the colonial policies of forced labor and conscription into the army. The revolt was quickly put down and its leaders hanged at Tominian.

In the western part of the country, a more protracted and religiously based form of resistance occurred over many years from 1923 until 1951. This resistance to colonial rule occurred among the Hamallists, members of a Tijani Moslem sect whose leader, Shaykh Mohammed al Tishiti Hamallah (1883–1943), lived at Nioro du Sahel. Hamallah inherited the leadership of the sect in 1909 when its Algerian founder, Sidi Mohammed bin Ahmed, died. In part, what differentiates the members of the sect from other Tijani is their recitation of a prayer of the Tijani litany eleven times instead of twelve and their use of an eleven-beaded rosary. Because of the latter, the French referred to the sect as *onze grains* (eleven grains).

Hamallah's appeal lay in his religious and mystic magnetism. Of great concern to the French colonial authorities was his appeal among educated Africans who used membership in the sect as a means of expressing anticolonial sentiment. In 1922–1923, violent confrontations took place between the Hamallists and other Moslems in Nioro. Finally, in 1925 the French exiled Hamallah to Mederdaa in Mauritania, not so much because of the violence in Nioro, but because of the rapid spread of the sect among African teachers and civil servants. His exile prompted more violent incidents, the worst occurring in Kaedi (Mauritania), where thirty people were killed. Hamallah was then moved to the Ivory Coast and eventually released in 1936.

Back in Nioro, his religious teachings constituted a threat to Tijani orthodoxy and to its leaders, who sought to exaggerate his danger to the French. In 1941, the Hamallists killed 6 Europeans in the main hotel in Bobo-Dioulasso (now Burkina Faso). In 1943, a severe conflict occurred between the Hamallists and other Tijani Moslems in which 400 people were killed, mostly women and children. Some 700 Hamallists were arrested, 33 were sentenced to death by firing squad, and Hamallah was deported to Algeria, where he died the same year. However, his movement continued to grow, serving as a vehicle for expressing opposition to colonial rule. After the establishment of political parties in 1946, the Hamalliya lost its appeal and since independence has had little appeal to younger Malians.[8]

Resistance to colonial rule also took less violent forms. Prominent among these was the 1947 strike of 5,000 railway workers in French West Africa. Labor leaders in Bamako played an important role in this strike.[9]

THE BIRTH OF POLITICAL PARTIES

Political leadership in French West Africa emerged among an African elite whose difference from the rest of the population was measured in education. Most had eight years of primary school training, and a smaller number went on to train at the Ecole William Ponty in Dakar. During the first thirty years of the twentieth century, the members of this educated elite occupied positions as clerks, teachers, and technicians. By the late 1930s, they began to organize into a number of voluntary associations whose stated purposes were social, cultural, and sportive. One of the principal movers of this movement was Mamby Sidibé (1891–1977), a schoolteacher, administrator, and writer. A political activist, he founded the Association des Lettrés, which brought the educated elite of the colony together, including men such as Mamadou Konaté and Modibo Keita who were to play important roles in Mali's political development. The French transferred Sidibé out of Bamako to Bandiagara in an attempt to stifle the movement.

Despite Sidibé's departure, the organization continued and others like it developed. Among these were Amicale Sportive de Bamako, Société-Sportive Soudanaise, Art et Travail, and Les Flamboyants. Members of the educated African elite often belonged to several of these groups, at which, besides engaging in social or cultural activities, they also discussed politics. Thus, the voluntary associations served to bring most of the elite from diverse ethnic groups into regular communication with one another. The presence of large numbers of Ponty alumni gave these associations commonality of purpose, created strong ties and a single purpose—eventual independence.[10]

In time, the French encouraged these associations to join a common grouping called the Maison du Peuple (People's House) and to use a meeting house of the same name. The Amis du Rassemblement Populaire du Soudan Français (ARP), a group of French colonial officials in the Sudan who supported the Popular Front government in France, helped establish the Maison du Peuple and promoted the development of voluntary associations. The colonial administration tried to control the voluntary associations through the ARP.

The year 1937 also witnessed the birth of trade unions in the French Sudan. Among the first of these was a teachers' union founded by Mamadou Konaté and his associates in the Association des Anciens Elèves du Lycée Terrasson de Fougères, the alumni association of the Sudan's secondary school, which was then a major voluntary association. The development of Konaté's trade union and other unions was made possible by the liberal policies and laws of the Popular Front.

Whereas the voluntary associations provided for networks among the elite, the trade unions were forums for communication between elite leaders and the urban masses. Unlike the voluntary associations, they provided the mass following necessary to create a nationalist movement.

The trade unions and voluntary associations did not unite people along ethnic lines. Those who moved to ever-growing and new urban agglomerations such as Bamako, where these organizations developed, soon found their kinship and ethnic ties weakened by physical distance, different social and economic concerns, and association with people from other ethnic groups. Membership in voluntary associations and unions provided urban dwellers with an opportunity to deal with shared concerns devoid of ethnic distinctions.[11] In a sense then, these new groupings represented multiethnic adaptations to change that borrowed the association strategies long used by traditional African societies. The absence of ethnic politics during this period and later in Mali's history can be traced to the fact that the new urban dwellers rallied around relevant current concerns and not around less relevant rural kinship ties.

The developments of the Popular Front era from 1936 to 1939 came to an end with strict wartime control of political activities. Although the Vichy government was successful in suppressing most voluntary association activity, elites in the French Sudan looked toward the future. The French Left enjoyed the respect of political elites in the French Sudan because of the role of the former in sponsoring the ARP and the Maison du Peuple. The French Communists also enjoyed a close relationship with African elites because they supported many of the demands of the latter for political reform. Around 1943, the Groupes d'Etudes Communistes (GEC) were formed in several West African cities, including Bamako. Led by French Communists, these groups discussed Marxism and the ways it could be used to solve African problems. After liberation in 1944, the Foyer du Soudan, an outgrowth of the Association des Lettrés, was formed. It was a union of voluntary associations in Bamako and as such became the springboard for the development of political parties.

The impetus for the formation of political parties came in August 1945, when Africans were able to participate in elections for the First Constituent Assembly of the Fourth Republic. Candidates without formal political party structures presented themselves in the following October elections. Among them was Fily Dabo Sissoko, a schoolteacher and *chef de canton*, who was an important man in the traditional society of the western area of the colony. This status, coupled with his conservative views, gave him the support of the French colonial administration. Mamadou Konaté, who enjoyed trade union support, was a candidate, as was Modibo Keita, who enjoyed the support of the radical GEC and the French Communists. None of the three candidates relied on ethnic support; rather, each relied on the appeal their views had for ethnically heterogeneous groups of voters.

An inconclusive election, forcing a run-off ballot, prompted the development of political groupings. Among these was the short-lived Parti Démocratique Soudanais (PDS), founded in 1945 by two French Communists, which supported Modibo Keita in the run-off election. That same year saw the development of the Bloc Soudanais, a political party founded by Mamadou Konaté and Modibo Keita after Fily Dabo Sissoko's election. Keita, realizing Konate's enormous personal appeal to enfranchised voters, was willing to subordinate his political views and take second place in order to remain politically viable. The Bloc Soudanais placed such great emphasis on unity that the name Union Soudanaise (US) was used interchangeably with Bloc Soudanais.

On the broader stage, the Brazzaville Conference (November-December 1944), convened by Gen. Charles de Gaulle, committed France to sweeping colonial reforms in all its colonies but avoided the issue of independence. In 1946, significant political divisions in the French Sudan became apparent with the development of the Parti Progressiste Soudanais (PPS) by Fily Dabo Sissoko's supporters. The Union Soudanaise became affiliated with the Rassemblement Démocratique Africain (RDA), an international political party established at a Bamako congress in October 1946 and led by Felix Houphouet-Boigny of the Ivory Coast. The US in effect became its Sudanese affiliate.[12] From 1946 to 1955, the RDA was affiliated with the French Communist party.

The PPS was supported by the colonial administration and represented the conservative elements and interests of Sudanese society. It aimed at increasing political autonomy, but in cooperation with France. The US, in contrast, put forth a strong anticolonialist ideology and encouraged hostility and opposition to colonial rule among the masses. It sought an abrupt break with the colonial power. As a result, the US was strongly opposed to the PPS. The PPS lost its dominance to the US in the 1956 National Assembly elections because of implementation of the *loi cadre* (framework law) granting universal suffrage, which gave the US expanded support. The *loi cadre* of 1956 contained other significant reforms in colonial administration, giving increased powers to territorial assemblies and weakening the governor-general of French West Africa.

THE MALI FEDERATION AND INDEPENDENCE

With his defeat at the polls in 1956, Fily Dabo Sissoko changed the name of the PPS to the Parti du Régroupement Soudanais, a strategy that failed to gain further support. Later, he and his followers joined the US-RDA, setting the stage for the French Sudan's achieving independence as a one-party state. Mamadou Konaté, who was the secretary-general of the US-RDA and the territory's leading political leader, died of liver cancer in 1956, making possible Modibo Keita's rise to power. On May 13, 1958, General de Gaulle returned to power in France, following the uprising in Algeria. On September 28, a referendum was held on the future status of the territories under the proposed constitution of the French Fifth Republic. In the proposal, de Gaulle gave African electorates a broad range of options about their future that included total integration with France, political autonomy within the French Community, and immediate independence. All except Guinea, which became independent, chose the second option. The Fifth Republic constitution, promulgated on October 5, created the French Community, dissolved the federation of French West Africa, and allowed states to group as they saw fit. Léopold Sédar Senghor of Senegal championed the idea of a united independent federation, as did Modibo Keita, who had become head of the government of the Sudanese Republic (République Soudanaise) that October.[13]

Although several territories initially expressed interest in federating, in the end only the Sudanese Republic and Senegal did, forming the Mali Federation, which obtained its independence from France on June 20, 1960. Modibo Keita became premier and head of state in the interim before the presidential elections scheduled for the following August. Keita and his followers sharply differed from the Senegalese on a number of key issues, including relations with France, Africanization of state services, and command of the armed forces. The Sudanese withdrew their support for Senghor's presidency of the federation, thus confronting him with the possibility of losing not only the federal presidency but also political power in Senegal.

Matters quickly came to a head on August 19, when the Sudanese mobilized the federal army and the Senegalese did the same with the gendarmerie. The latter rapidly got the upper hand in Dakar, and on August 22, Modibo Keita and his associates were sent in a sealed train to Bamako. The Senegalese territorial assembly rapidly voted for independence, as did the Sudanese shortly thereafter.[14]

NONETHNIC POLITICS
AND THE RISE OF MODIBO KEITA

The development of political parties in the Sudan was not along ethnic lines, contrary to the case in many countries of Africa. The Malian parties developed among urban dwellers, principally those living in Bamako, where shared social and economic concerns overshadowed rural ethnic ties. Thus, what distinguished the parties was not ethnicity but ideology and objectives. The most radical of the politicians was Modibo Keita, who initially was a minor player compared to Fily Dabo Sissoko and Mamadou Konaté. The latter's death in 1956 opened the way for Modibo Keita, who had previously moved over from the smaller radical GEC into the number-two position in the US-RDA. This wise political move together with Konaté's death gave Keita the leadership of the US-RDA. His only political rival was Sissoko, who in time also joined the US-RDA. By 1958, Keita was the territory's leading political leader, appealing to most levels of society and to all ethnic groups because of his militant stance against colonialism and promise of better things to come with independence.

4

Malian Politics
Since Independence

Although the Mali Federation effectively broke up on August 20, 1960, Modibo Keita continued efforts to preserve the federation throughout the following weeks. He employed a variety of strategies, including a visit to President de Gaulle in Paris, a threat of breaking diplomatic relations with any countries extending diplomatic relations to Senegal, and an appeal to the United Nations. A state of siege was declared throughout the Sudanese Republic, and it was in this highly charged atmosphere that an extraordinary congress of the US-RDA took place in Bamako and declared the country's independence on September 22, 1960, as the Republic of Mali. The border with Senegal was closed, and train service between the two countries stopped for what would turn out to be a three-year period.

During the brief era of the Sudanese Republic, the basis of local administration was established in Mali. Six regions were created: Kayes, Bamako, Ségou, Sikasso, Mopti, and Gao, each headed by a governor reporting to the minister of the interior. The 6 regions were in turn divided into 42 *cercles*, which were subdivided into 228 arrondissements. As in the colonial era, the *cercles* were headed by commandants. The headquarters of *cercles* were large villages or towns, which had police, health, education, and justice services. An arrondissement groups several villages and its *chef* (head) is responsible for collecting taxes, recording births and deaths, performing marriages, and settling local disputes.

The administrative reforms of 1977 divided the Gao region into two, Gao and Timbuctoo, created 50 additional arrondissements, 4 new *cercles*, and established an autonomous district of Bamako, surrounding the capital. During the Keita era, regional assemblies existed, but functioned only irregularly, and were later dissolved.[1] In 1989, there were 281 arrondissements.

THE PRESIDENCY OF MODIBO KEITA

Modibo Keita, Mali's first president, was born in Bamako in 1915. A graduate of the Ecole William Ponty in Dakar, he was a schoolteacher who became a political activist. In 1945, he and Mamadou Konaté founded the Bloc Soudanais political party, which eventually merged with the broader West African political grouping, the Rassemblement Démocratique Africain. Keita's political alliances in Mali and French-speaking West Africa were forged among his fellow William Ponty alumni. His political support came from a broad array of urban dwellers. In 1947, he was elected to the territorial assembly of the Sudan and from 1956 to 1958 served as a deputy and vice president of the French National Assembly.

Early in his political career, Keita solidified his association with the French Communist party. He was a prominent member of the Groupes d'Etudes Communistes and was the candidate of the PDS in the 1945 Constituent Assembly run-off elections. The GEC and the PDS were founded and supported by French Communists, and their adherents believed that Marxism could be used to solve African problems. A dedicated Marxist, Keita tried to adapt its principles to Malian conditions. His economic objective was a state-run economy patterned on those in the Soviet Union and in Eastern Europe, and his political goal was a one-party Marxist state.

Modibo Keita was both president of the republic and secretary of the US-RDA. A charismatic leader, he forged a highly centralized form of government, quickly Africanized the civil service, and reaffirmed the *options socialistes* (socialist options), which he had originally put forth for the Mali Federation. Marxism became the guiding political philosophy for Keita's administration, resulting in a state-run economy and close diplomatic ties with Communist and socialist governments throughout the world. A National Assembly, a descendant of the previous colonial territorial assembly, was established at independence. Its seventy-eight delegates—all belonging to the US-RDA—were elected for five-year terms, and during Keita's presidency only two such elections were held. The president of the National Assembly during the Keita era was Mahamane Alassane Haidara, who was from Timbuctoo, in the northeast. A schoolteacher and an Ecole William Ponty graduate, he shared many of Keita's political views and served as a major link for Keita to the populations of Mali's north.

Keita forged the US-RDA as a mass party that also had the support of the country's principal regional political leaders. These regional leaders included Haidara, representing the Songhay; Yacouba Maiga, from An-songo in the extreme east of the country, also representing the Songhay;

Mali's first president, Modibo Keita (photo courtesy of Ministry of Information, Mali)

and Somine Dolo from Sanga, representing the Dogon. The US-RDA had absorbed all opposition political parties and most voluntary organizations such as labor unions, women's organizations, youth groups, and even the veteran's organization. Thus, there were no organized groups outside of the party structure capable of expressing political dissent.

In a move to strengthen his position, Keita had the National Assembly reconfirm him as president in January 1961. That year, he announced an austerity program and unveiled Mali's first five-year development program. In July 1961, Keita announced that Mali would leave the West African Monetary Union and issue its own currency, the Malian franc. This nonconvertible national currency was issued on July 1, 1962. Its issuance in Bamako was followed on July 20 by a riot of traders and merchants whose regional trade was effectively destroyed by a nonconvertible currency. Following the riot, the Keita government ordered the arrest of Fily Dabo Sissoko, Hamadoun Dicko, and Kassoum Touré. Sissoko had been Keita's preindependence political archrival. Sissoko, Dicko, and Touré, along with ninety-five others, were charged with treason and attempting a coup in the Mali franc riot and tried by a "popular tribunal" outside of the established judicial system. Sissoko was condemned to death, a sentence later commuted to life imprisonment at hard labor.

In arresting Sissoko and his associates, Keita eliminated a potential source of political challenge to his authority. Sissoko, Dicko, and Touré were sent to the *cercle* of Kidal in the northeast, where a rebellion among the Tuareg was in progress. Shortly thereafter it was rumored in Bamako that they had been shot, and their supporters charged Keita with political assassination. Almost two years later, in August 1964, the National Political Bureau of the US-RDA issued a statement explaining that the three had been killed in a Tuareg ambush while being taken by truck to Bouressa near the Algerian border. Most Malians have never accepted this explanation; it is popularly held that the three men were executed on orders from the Keita government.[2]

Keita ruthlessly eliminated all forms of dissent. When the people of the Bambara village of Sakoiba protested against his policies, its inhabitants were arrested, others invited to take their possessions, and the village physically leveled to the ground.

Just prior to the Mali franc riot, the Tuareg in northeastern Mali, supported with arms and supplies from Morocco and Algeria, rebelled against the new government. Keita initially accused the French of backing the rebels and later was successful in getting both Morocco and Algeria to help in putting the rebellion down through aerial bombardment of encampments and poisoning of wells. The Tuareg rebellion was finally ended in late 1964.

In April 1964, the US-RDA presented a slate of candidates for election to the National Assembly. Keita's socialist options had, by this time, become unpopular with large segments of Malian society. Although he almost completely Africanized government bureaucracy and a large number of state-owned companies provided employment to many, the nonconvertible currency, the lack of hard currency reserves, and the disincentives to farmer productivity created by a state marketing board and collectivization led to food shortages and scarcities of consumer products. Not surprisingly, the black market and smuggling thrived in this economic environment.

Keita dealt with popular unrest over his policies by denouncing the forces of counterrevolution. In March 1965, a Comité National de Défense de la Révolution (CNDR) was created; its members included US-RDA Marxist hard-liners such as Ousmane Ba, foreign minister; Seydou Badian Kouyaté, minister of development and the US-RDA's Marxist theoretician; Madeira Keita, minister of defense; and Col. Sékou Traoré, army chief of staff. The CNDR remained relatively inactive until August 1967.

During 1965 and 1966, Keita's government was plagued by serious economic and financial difficulties that eventually led to monetary negotiations with France. These talks resulted in monetary accords signed on February 15, 1967, in which France agreed to support the Mali franc, which was devalued 50 percent on May 5. Mali agreed not only to the devaluation but also to cutting government expenditures. The moderates in Keita's government, such as Jean-Marie Koné, minister of state in charge of planning and coordination of economic and financial affairs, and Louis Nègre, minister of finance and governor of the Banque de la République du Mali, had convinced Keita of the need for these accords.

However, the Marxist radicals in the government viewed the accords as a violation of basic party principles. In order to appease the latter, to remain true to his own socialist principles, and to energize the political life of the country, Keita embarked on a series of radical initiatives that made his government widely unpopular. In a nationally aired radio speech, he announced the dissolution of the National Political Bureau of the US-RDA and the assumption of authority over the government and party by the CNDR. In his radio address, Keita stated that the CNDR's objective was the political and economic cleansing of Mali and the preparation of conditions conducive for receiving the political direction of the US-RDA.

Keita and his supporters had prepared the public for these radical changes during the previous weeks through a series of carefully orchestrated demonstrations of support by youth groups, the army, and labor unions. Five months later, in January 1968, the National Assembly dissolved itself and authorized Keita to appoint a legislative delegation. The Popular Militia of 3,000 young men was reactivated, and following the tactics of their model, the Red Guards in Mao's China, set out to uncover corruption and to purify the party.

Keita and his followers raised their restructuring and cleansing operation to a fever pitch through the use of fiery rhetoric and the establishment of local committees for the defense of the revolution. Rooting out corruption and mismanagement in both the party and the government also provided Keita with visible scapegoats who could be blamed for the country's many economic ills. At the same time, Keita himself was deified in slogans, the newspapers, in official pronouncements by other officials, and in song by the country's traditional singers as the supreme guide of the revolution and as Le Guide Eclairé. The criminal conviction of once-powerful party and government officials pleased the public for a while but had little staying power in explaining all of the country's ills. Many who doubted the soundness of Keita's basic socialist options were swiftly punished for even minimal expressions of dissent.

The Popular Militia manned roadblocks, conducted searches of home and person at will, detained many on the least pretext, and engaged in torture. The militia rapidly became the most hated element of Keita's Cultural Revolution. The excesses of the militia affected the personal liberties of many and in practical terms, it became a terror to ordinary citizens. By late 1968, there was widespread discontent with Keita and his policies, not mobilized into a political force capable of overthrowing his regime, but constituting a favorable background against which a coup d'état could take place.

During 1968, significant strains developed between the army and the militia. Equal in size to the army's 3,000 men, the poorly trained militia was particularly irritating to a number of young army officers who had been personally harassed by it. A group of them asked Keita to disband the militia or to place it under army control. He refused to do either, and it was widely believed in army circles that he planned instead to arrest a number of army officers on November 20, 1968, after his return from a conference in Mopti. All of these elements, plus the ambitions of a group of army officers to seize power for themselves, led to Keita's eventual overthrow.

THE COUP D'ÉTAT
OF NOVEMBER 19, 1968

Yoro Diakité, an army captain who was the director of the Inter-Services School at Kati, had sensed that the time was nearing when the public would rally behind a military coup d'état. Diakité and his fellow officers saw such an act not only as a means of ridding Mali of the abuses of Keita's regime but also as an opportunity to seize power. Diakité apparently lacked the resolve to carry out the coup and procrastinated. However, word of the planned coup reached Keita and a number of Diakité's subordinate coplotters believed that they would be arrested on the president's return from Mopti. The move for an immediate coup was promoted by Lt. Moussa Traoré, an instructor at the Kati school, where a number of junior officers supported him. Traoré's timing was dictated by fears of his own imminent arrest and that of his fellow officers. As Traoré seized the leadership initiative, Diakité was relegated to the number-two position.

The coup d'état of November 19, 1968, was carried out in an almost bloodless manner in the early morning hours. President Keita was returning on the riverboat *General Soumaré* from a regional economic meeting in Mopti when word reached him that army units had seized key installations in Bamako. Confident that he could reverse these events through an appeal to the public, he disembarked as planned several hours later at Koulikoro and drove on to Bamako. He was arrested en route. Members of the government, the CNDR, and the Popular Militia were also taken into custody. At noon, Traoré announced the fall of the "dictatorial regime of Modibo Keita" and the formation of the Comité Militaire de Liberation Nationale (CMLN). The following day, massive street demonstrations took place in support of the coup, and people shouted "down with Modibo; down with the militia."[3] Significantly, no one shouted "down with socialism" because so many urban dwellers were the beneficiaries of the secure employment afforded by Keita's socialist policies.

The US-RDA and the CNDR were quickly abolished, and a provisional government was announced three days later with Diakité as its head. Diakité also served as first vice president of the CMLN. Moussa Traoré became chief of state and president of the CMLN. On December 6, most of the provisions of the constitution of 1960 were abrogated and replaced by a Fundamental Law under which Mali was governed until 1974, when a new constitution was approved. The Fundamental Law interpreted the powers of the CMLN and its composition, defined the new government, and stated which provisions of the 1960 constitution were still in effect. Traoré eventually replaced Diakité as head of the government.

The principal losers in the 1968 coup were Keita and his political supporters. The army was the clear beneficiary, since it gained control of the state and its entire apparatus. Ordinary citizens also benefited from tangible improvements in personal liberties, the dissolution of the oppressive Popular Militia, which had made their lives miserable, and a relaxation in Keita's rigid state-run economy.

RULE OF THE MILITARY COMMITTEE
OF NATIONAL LIBERATION, 1968–1979

The military committee was initially composed of fourteen members. Many of them shared bonds of friendship from their days at the Kati Inter-Services School or at military camps and were from the western region of Kayes, and a number were of Khassonke origins. However, regional and ethnic affinities figured less significantly than the collegial ones established through experiences in military service. None of the members of the CMLN was known to the Malian public. Most were extremely inexperienced in administration and of modest intellectual ability. Moussa Traoré, the committee's president, was presented to the public over Radio Mali as an experienced administrator, although that was clearly not true. A graduate of the Fréjus Military College in France, Traoré returned to Mali in 1960, was promoted to lieutenant in 1964, and was an instructor at the Inter-Services School from 1964 to 1968, serving under Capt. Yoro Diakité. Diakité, the more experienced senior officer, and three other captains, Malik Diallo, Mamadou Sissoko, and Charles Samba Sissoko, took leadership positions in the new government. However, real power rested with the aggressive young lieutenants who had masterminded the coup.

The CMLN established as its principal objective the correction of the flawed economic policies of the Keita regime. Of significance was the fact that the CMLN did not reject in rhetoric or practice Keita's socialist options. Instead, it blamed him for failing to make economic programs work in the public interest. The CMLN had little choice but to retain Keita's state-run economy, not the least because so many urban dwellers were employed in it. The committee's new domestic policy directions had enormous mass appeal; they included greater individual freedoms, the encouragement of private traders, the dismantling of collectivized agriculture, the removal of internal customs controls, the dissolution of compulsory Marxist political indoctrination sessions and compulsory attendance at political rallies, the abolition of the many indirect taxes that went into supporting the party, and the dissolution of the paramilitary and parapolitical bodies that had been created in violation of the constitution.

The CMLN promised a quick return of civilian rule, but there were sharp differences of opinion on this issue among the fourteen members of the group. In the early days, there was little pressure for a return to civilian rule from the Malian public, which was more than satisfied with

President Moussa Traoré with hand raised, 1971 (photo by author)

the CMLN's short-term accomplishments. The pragmatic policies of the CMLN not only guaranteed employment for the urban elites in the government bureaucracy or in parastatals as Keita had done but also provided all Malians with a market full of long-desired imported consumer goods, a substantial amount of freedom, and hope for the future. In rural areas, the dissolution of Keita's bureaucratic apparatus for the collectivization of agriculture helped win the CMLN the support of the masses.

Malian politics during the early years of the CMLN were characterized by power struggles within the committee and by external challenges to its rule by dissident elements within the military and by various civilian groups including students, teachers, and unions.[4] Early on, friction arose between Yoro Diakité, president of the provisional government, and Moussa Traoré. Diakité's personal ambition, together with his political views favoring closer ties to the West and France, made open conflict inevitable. Diakité was eventually demoted, becoming minister of transport, telecommunication, and tourism, and in 1971 was accused along with Malik Diallo, another member of the CMLN, of plotting a coup. Both were expelled from the CMLN, and on July 31, 1972, were sentenced to life imprisonment with hard labor. Both died in prison in 1973. The removal of Diakité and Diallo and the death in an auto accident of Mamadou Sissoko in 1969 reduced the CMLN membership to eleven.

In April 1969, students at the Ecole Normale Supérieure struck, vowing support for the Keita regime. This was followed in July by further student strikes, which were rapidly crushed by the CMLN. The following August, the first of several coup attempts against Moussa Traoré was uncovered. It was alleged that a coup d'état had been planned for August 14, 1969, by Capt. Diby Silas Diarra, one of Modibo Keita's most trusted military officers, who had played a prominent role in suppressing the Tuareg rebellion of the early 1960s. It was also alleged that Diarra and his coconspirators planned to reinstate Keita. Diarra was sentenced to life in prison at hard labor on December 14, 1969, and sent to the salt mines at Taoudeni. He died in prison the following year after losing sight in one eye.[5]

From 1969 through 1971, the CMLN faced challenges from trade unionists whose Union Nationale des Travailleurs du Mali (UNTM) was dissolved by the Fundamental Law of 1968. Union leaders, who had been activists in the now outlawed US-RDA, found themselves with a reduced voice in the affairs of the country and were largely proponents of Keita's socialist policies, some of which the CMLN had scuttled. Matters came to a head in October 1970, when a congress of the reconstituted UNTM openly challenged the CMLN's rule and told its members to return to their barracks. Early the next year, the CMLN rejected the new statutes of the UNTM, dissolved its provisional consultative committee, and jailed thirty trade unionists, who were released two months later.

The CMLN continued to use consensus as its operational basis. After the removal of Diakité and Diallo, the power core consisted of Moussa Traoré and six others, including Filifing Sissoko, Traoré's closest ally and the committee's theoretician. The others included Kissima Doukara, who headed the ministries of defense, interior, and security; Tiecoro Bagayoko, director of security services; Baba Diarra, vice president of the CMLN and minister of finance and commerce as well as of education and development planning at various periods; Youssouf Traoré, minister of information; and Charles Samba Sissoko, minister of foreign affairs.[6]

Support for Keita and his policies was obviously strong during the early years of the CMLN's rule. In part, this was due to the almost guaranteed state employment Keita's policies provided for many. This, coupled with the highly politicized nature of the country's cadres, required that the CMLN move cautiously in changing course and in neutralizing Keita's supporters. The latter was achieved by keeping the upper cadres of Keita's regime in detention and by assigning US-RDA officials to

Independence Day parade, 1971, slogan (long live the people's anti-imperialist struggle) (photo by author)

provincial posts, where military officers occupied most of the governorships and commanded the important *cercles*. Fear that the old Keita guard might work its way back into power heightened as the CMLN prepared a new constitution. During the same period, the early 1970s, the CMLN also had to deal with a severe drought in the Sahelian area of the country that left 80,000 refugees, most of them members of nomadic groups.

THE CONSTITUTION OF 1974

On June 2, 1974, the CMLN presented a new constitution, which was approved by over 99 percent of the electorate. There is no evidence that large-scale fraud occurred. In fact, most Malians were pleased to vote for the constitution, as its provisions had broad political appeal. Many of its provisions are similar to those of the 1960 constitution, but there are differences. The constitution provides for a single political party, universal suffrage, election of a president for five-year terms (later changed to six-year terms), and a National Assembly, whose members are elected for four years (changed by a 1981 amendment to three years). It barred from party membership and participation in the government and the National Assembly for a period of ten years all those who had held leading positions in the US-RDA and Keita's government. It also provided that the CMLN conduct the affairs of the country for another five years, until 1979, which it did.

The new constitution enabled the CMLN to move forward toward civilian rule. However, elements within the committee, led by Doukara and Bagayoko, essentially opposed this move, seeing it as a threat to their power and perquisites. As director of Mali's drought relief effort and coordinator of all foreign aid for drought victims, Doukara had become a powerful figure in Mali, second only to the president. Bagayoko, because he was director of security services, was also powerful. Some of Keita's supporters characterized Traoré's promise of a return to civilian rule as a charade in which the military would simply put on civilian clothes. Despite these external criticisms and the opposition within the CMLN, Traoré moved ahead with a course that would ultimately legitimate his rule.

RETURN TO CIVILIAN RULE UNDER
A MILITARY-SPONSORED POLITICAL PARTY

On September 22, 1975, Moussa Traoré announced plans for the formation of a new political party. The following January, in his New Year's address, Traoré announced that the new party's role would be to mobilize people in the creation of an independent economy. The new party's statutes were drafted by Filifing Sissoko, who was the permanent secretary of the CMLN. The proposed statutes were vigorously debated within the CMLN, with opposition led by Doukara and Bagayoko. Finally, on September 26, 1976, the statutes were made public, and early the next year members of the CMLN visited the country's regions to explain the new political order. The new party, called the Union Démocratique du Peuple Malien (UDPM), was greeted with little enthusiasm by a public that had been wearied by the oppressive, intrusive, and costly activities of the old US-RDA. The UDPM is organized along Marxist-Leninist lines and heavily borrows from Modibo Keita's principle of democratic centralism, yet it is not a Marxist party.[7]

Students in Bamako used the informational meetings organized to explain the new party as a forum to protest new post–secondary school examinations for entry into university and technical school training. Schools were closed and students jailed. Those on the CMLN who were opposed to civilian rule had their position strengthened by these disturbances, interpreting them as the public response to gestures toward democratic government.

However, Traoré and other members of the CMLN saw that the country's youth would become increasingly disaffected, as would junior military officers, if democratization did not move ahead quickly. In fall 1977, CMLN members again visited the regions in order to set up the party apparatus. As a gesture of reconciliation, the CMLN had released fifteen of Keita's closest political allies in June 1975, and six more five months later. Finally, in February 1977, Keita, who had been held at Kidal in the northeast, was transferred to Bamako, supposedly to prepare him for release in what some claim was to be a gesture of national reconciliation. Keita suddenly died on May 16, 1977, and many suspected that he had been secretly murdered by lethal injection or by poisoning.[8] In an attempt to dispel these rumors, President Traoré announced on June 6, 1977, that the former president had died of a lung infection. Keita's funeral on May 18, 1977, was the occasion for a large-scale anti-CMLN demonstration by teachers, students, and former supporters. The CMLN responded by arresting several hundred people, most of whom were released several months later.

Despite these setbacks, President Traoré moved ahead with putting the UDPM apparatus in place. Party elections in 1977 firmly established this apparatus. It consists of a Central Executive Bureau (Bureau Executif Central) (BEC) of 19 members, and a National Council of 137 members. Structures at the regional, *cercle*, and arrondissement level were put in place as well. The firm establishment of the party cleared the way for elections for a civilian government whose president was clearly going to be Moussa Traoré, who was secretary-general of the UDPM.

In a further gesture of reconciliation, the CMLN released Keita's widow in January 1978 and other political prisoners as well. Doukara, Bagayoko, and their supporters saw civilian rule as inevitable and with it the dissolution of the CMLN and an end to their hold on power. They plotted to assassinate the president and seize power. Their attempt failed, and on February 28, 1978, the two leaders were arrested along with Karim Dembélé, another member of the CMLN, and other officers.[9] The following month, Charles Samba Sissoko, a CMLN member and minister of foreign affairs, was arrested for complicity in the plot. Both Doukara and Bagayoko were sentenced to death by the State Security Court on October 21, 1978, and Dembélé and Sissoko given prison terms. All four were tried a second time in 1979 for corruption, Doukara being accused of having embezzled $9 million in drought-relief funds. Both Doukara and Bagayoko died at the Taoudeni salt mines in 1983. In a related event, Joseph Mara, a CMLN member and minister of justice, who was serving as president of a national commission investigating corruption of the CMLN members arrested in 1978, was himself arrested on January 2, 1979, for corruption. He was sentenced by the State Security Court on March 8, 1979, to twenty years at hard labor.

These events effectively removed all internal CMLN opposition to civilian rule, eliminated the Soviet influence on the committee that operated through the four deposed officers, and reduced the size of the committee from its original fourteen to six. Karim Dembélé and several other officers arrested in the 1978 coup attempt were pardoned and released from the Taoudeni salt mine prison in September 1988. At that time, President Traoré, who pardoned or commuted the sentences of seventy-eight prisoners held at Taoudeni, announced that the prison was being closed down.

On June 19, 1979, general elections were held for the presidency and eighty-two seats in the National Assembly. All UDPM candidates were elected by an overwhelming majority. Moussa Traoré, after almost eleven years as president, was formally elected to the position for the first time by the electorate. The CMLN was formally dissolved on June 28, 1979, with four of its members joining the Central Executive Bureau of the UDPM, and two retiring.

MALI'S CIVILIAN GOVERNMENT
AND ITS CHALLENGES

Although President Traoré's detractors continued to mutter that Mali still had military rule in civilian garb, it was obvious that he had greatly broadened civilian representation in government and had given the public access to the electoral process. Traoré was reelected to a second six-year term as president on June 9, 1985, by 99.94 percent of voters. In that election, 82 UDPM candidates were elected (including 47 incumbents), 3 of whom were women, to the National Assembly for three-year terms. National Assembly elections were again held on June 26, 1988. More than one candidate was allowed to run on the UDPM ticket for each National Assembly seat. This gave the impression of a contested election, allowed voters to express their displeasure and anger with government by turning out incumbents, and crippled the prospects of most candidates for building up personal political power bases through the electoral process. Forty of the 82 members elected in June 1988 were newcomers, and a total of 5 women were elected or reelected. The government set up 2,647 polling stations for the 1988 elections, in which 97.9 percent of the 3,701,006 registered voters voted. Blank votes were cast by 4,742 voters.

Legislative elections in Mali under the UDPM have served several useful purposes for Moussa Traoré and his government. They provide for limited participation in government by the public, represent a democratic process for the international community, and allow voters to use the voting booths instead of the streets to vent their anger and frustration.

That almost half of incumbents were turned out in both the 1985 and 1988 elections is a good barometer that voter dissatisfaction levels are high. National Assembly delegates are easy targets for a dissatisfied electorate and ready scapegoats for Traoré and his military supporters. Thus, Traoré and his principal military supporters are major beneficiaries of this electoral process. Still, the National Assembly plays an important role in policy formulation, and its members exert a fair degree of political influence. The presence of an elected National Assembly provides for public participation in government and satisfies to a degree popular wishes for a say in the country's political affairs.

Traoré's domestic policies were shaped through consensus within the CMLN in the 1968–1979 period. Since 1979, they have been shaped within the UDPM leadership, which includes some of the president's old military colleagues. Traoré has relied on pragmatism and international and bilateral economic aid to deal with Mali's greatest domestic policy issue, its poor economy. He has also relied on the BEC and the congresses of the UDPM to support his policies.

Turning away from Keita's socialist domestic policies has been slow because the urban elite, who dominate the political process, are primarily employed by the government or the parastatals and their salaries consume 80 percent of the annual operating budget. In 1985, the Malian government employed close to 50,000 civil servants and 15,000 in the parastatals, having added close to 5,000 annually to the former during the 1970s. Attempts to reform the system sparked an inevitable confrontation with those who saw their expected entitlements jeopardized, notably students and teachers. These confrontations occurred, however, after Traoré had solidified his power by establishing a semblance of civilian rule. The student and teacher strikes of 1979 and 1980 were a serious political challenge to Traoré's rule. He met this challenge by judiciously using compromise, armed force, and political process in which many in UDPM leadership positions were faulted and removed. As a consequence, Traoré emerged relatively unscathed.

The stage was set for these confrontations in 1979 when Traoré's government sought to stem the flow of graduates of upper-level schools into the civil service and the parastatals, where previously 90 percent of them found employment. First the government denied employment to large numbers of graduates and then required two years of prior military service as a prerequisite for government employment. Simultaneously, the government sought to stem the flow of students into higher educational levels. In addition, the government withdrew student *bourses* (financial support) and failed to meet the civil service payroll because it simply did not have the necessary funds. This led to a galvanizing of student and teacher interests that resulted in a series of violent confrontations with the government between November 1979 and November 1980.

Students expressed their real anger through the guise of ideological disagreement with Traoré's new policy of an independent and planned national economy. Claiming their support for scientific socialism and the right to form their own independent association, they voted to strike on November 16, 1979, in response to a government announcement that new, tougher examinations would be given for entrance into professional training, a move intended to disqualify as many as possible for eventual government employment. Three hundred students were arrested and conscripted into the army. On December 17–18, 1979, even more violent demonstrations occurred and fifteen students were killed by police. In order to quell the riots, the government gave in to some of the student demands and promised to restore *bourses* and suspend the tougher examinations.

The student-led antigovernment protest was organized within the Union Nationale des Etudiants et des Elèves du Mali (UNEEM), an independent association formed in January 1979 and immediately proscribed by the government. Teachers, seeing the gains made by the students, were angered over their low salaries paid several months late and poor working conditions and established the Commission des Comités Syndicaux des Enseignants (CCSE) in the Bamako area. By January 1980, the government had given in to enough student and teacher demands to permit the opening of upper-level schools, some of which had been closed for a year. The Central Executive Bureau of the UDPM voted to have the government retroactively pay student *bourses* amounting to 1.4 billion Malian francs, money the government did not have. The following day, the UDPM decreed that all UNEEM committees in schools would be replaced by those of its own youth movement. The UNEEM committees had continued to function even though the organization had been proscribed by the government the previous year. This badly timed move and the news that the government could not meet the financial commitments made by the UDPM led to a student and teacher boycott of classes.

The boycott escalated into a sequence of almost constant student demonstrations throughout February 1980. Massive arrests of students and teachers followed. That month, a new secretary-general of the outlawed UNEEM was elected. Abdul Karim Camara, known as "Cabral," was to become a folk hero to protesting students. On March 8, 1980, he organized a "peaceful" demonstration in Bamako where the summit meeting of Saharan states opened. His attempt to embarrass the government led to a violent confrontation with police in which thirteen students were killed. Camara was arrested and died in custody. President

Traoré, wishing to deescalate the confrontation, granted clemency to arrested students on March 29, 1980, and released them from custody. The March confrontation effectively destroyed UNEEM; a combination of government promises of paying *bourses* and easing up on the examinations, together with student fears of reprisals, led to the demise of the protest movement.

Teachers, disgruntled by low wages and the government's failure to pay them regularly, launched another protest movement. Initially they refused to monitor student examinations, and they held a peaceful gathering commemorating the death of Abdul Karim Camara. The detention of these teachers led to a teacher's strike for ten days in October 1980. Teacher and student protests continued for several more months but eventually faded because of further government concessions and firm action.

President Traoré, sensing danger in all these events, announced in October that the UDPM had to be revitalized. This was an attempt on his part to shift the responsibility for the student-teacher troubles from himself to certain individuals within the UDPM leadership. His fears were well founded: In February 1981 the government announced that a group of fifteen gendarmes had plotted to assassinate the president on New Year's Eve. All were arrested and three sentenced to death.

An extraordinary congress of the UDPM was held in February 1981 and called for a liberalization of the economy and the abolition of numerous parastatals. A year later, the UDPM was revitalized at a regular congress, and eight of the nineteen members of the Central Executive Bureau were replaced. The ouster of 40 percent of the membership of the UDPM's Central Executive Bureau provided Traoré with breathing space from his domestic political troubles. Again, scapegoating others satisfied disgruntled elements of the population.

At the 1983 congress of the party, President Traoré encouraged Malians to seek employment in the private sector and the UDPM's national council called for a cutback in state employment. At that time he had no choice, given Mali's then almost complete reliance on French financial subsidies to support the civil service and its dependence on other donors to prop up its economy. During the 1980s, Mali received annual amounts of financial aid greater than its own internally raised revenues. Responding to the government's austerity policies, the World Bank, United Nations (UN) agencies, and the European Economic Community pledged $200 million for Mali's new five-year development program. France then forgave $10 million of Mali's pre-1978 debts. These were important gestures toward Traoré's government and served to bolster his political position.

In February 1984, Mali obtained readmission to the West African Monetary Union, and on June 1 the CFA franc replaced the Mali franc as the official currency. Mali's efforts to gain readmission to the union had been consistently blocked for a number of years by Upper Volta (Burkina Faso), motivated by the unresolved border dispute with Mali.

POLITICS IN THE LATE 1980s

President Traoré was reelected in 1985 by over 98 percent of the voters. The principal political issue was the government's Economic Reform Policy, whose major aim was to promote private enterprise, privatize a number of state enterprises, reform the commercial code, restructure the national budget, and make the country self-sufficient in food production. A 1985 congress of the UDPM called for the creation of a national fund to support self-sufficiency in food production (Fond National pour Autosuffisance Alimentaire). President Traoré and his government took a number of bold initiatives in this direction, particularly after 1985, prodded in part by the World Bank, the International Monetary Fund, and other donors, that also provided incentives. The United States alone gave Mali $18 million in aid linked to privatization efforts and reform of the commercial code.

There was significant political risk in this course of action, given Mali's low standard of living and the fact that privatization collided with the vested interests of an overinflated bureaucracy, parastatals, and educated youth, whose predecessors had enjoyed virtually guaranteed employment after graduation.

In June 1986 the president made major changes in his cabinet that underscored his commitment to the free enterprise option. They also signaled to Malians and international aid donors that the president meant to avoid the concentration of ministerial power for long periods in a few hands. Alioune Blondin-Beye, who had been minister of foreign affairs for eight years and a candidate for the post of secretary-general of the Organization of African Unity, was dropped and replaced by Modibo Keita (no relation to the former president), the former minister of employment and public function. Sékou Ly, formerly minister of education and the former mayor of both Nioro and Bamako, became minister of defense. The new position of prime minister was established and the president's personal physician and a former minister of public health, Mamadou Dembélé, was appointed to it. Although many viewed the prime minister's role as only one of coordination because the president remained head of the government, the creation of the post demonstrated the president's intent to revitalize the political life of the country by sharing power. To gain the support of Mali's women, a woman was appointed minister of public health, joining the other woman in the cabinet, the minister of information and telecommunications. The removal at this time of several long-time ministers who were also top party leaders further emphasized the president's desire to expand power sharing.[10]

A month following this major cabinet reshuffle, President Traoré made changes in the command of the armed forces, replacing Lt. Col. Koké Dembélé, who was then the chief of staff, with Lt. Col. Ousmane Coulibaly. The chief of staff of the Gendarmerie was also replaced.

As was the case with the US-RDA, the UDPM under Traoré encompasses regional political figures and most voluntary organizations in the country: women's groups, labor unions, youth groups, and the veterans' organization. This virtually eliminates the possibility of political dissent arising from any legitimately constituted group in the country. However, it does not remove possible challenges from proscribed groups either at home or abroad.

During summer 1986, President Traoré set out additional government priorities, including the attainment of food self-sufficiency, an objective put forth at the 1985 party congress, the fight against desertification and drought, and the need to reforest vast areas of the country. Both the emphasis on such measures by international donors and the effects of the 1984–1985 drought, when the Niger River at Bamako stopped flowing for the first time in recorded history, contributed to Traoré's announcing these priorities.

By the late 1980s, Mali's new administrative and economic frameworks were well in place. The emphasis in the balanced 1987 budget, for example, was on reducing personnel in government employment, providing incentives to private business, and orienting the activities of private business toward grass roots development. The drive toward free enterprise and the dismantling of unprofitable parastatals produced a predictable outcry from vested interest groups, notably students and labor unions. The government's chronic inability to meet its monthly payroll through both incompetence and corruption as well as intentional delays due to cash flow problems, became a major political issue in 1987 and 1988. Student protestors were treated firmly and fairly, but their arrest was consistently used by the Paris-based opposition in exile, the Committee for the Defense of Democratic Liberties in Mali, as a vehicle for attacking the Traoré government.

Corruption, because it plays a role in the government's inability to pay its employees on time, became a major political liability, one requiring action. In 1986, a UDPM congress adopted a national charter to encourage the "moralization of public life" and established a seventeen-member special commission, headed by UDPM Secretary Djibril Diallo, to assist in the anticorruption campaign. The objective of the charter and the commission was to deal with nepotism, absenteeism, corruption, and inefficiency. In February 1987, President Traoré appointed Soumana Sacko as minister of finance and trade and gave him a mandate to root out corruption. The thirty-seven-year-old minister soon became a folk hero to ordinary Malians because of the drastic measures he used to fight fraud and tax evasion. He successfully broke up an organized car-smuggling ring and recovered 577 vehicles that had been illegally cleared through customs. At the same time, he fired senior officials in his own ministry and at the state-owned Mali Development Bank, accusing them of corruption.

Sacko promised prompt payment of salaries that were generally paid several months late. He delivered in part on this promise by freezing a number of government expenditures not specified by law, abolishing hardship and official travel allowances within the country, and cracking down on corruption and inefficiency. This won for him the nickname of "minister of salaries" among government employees. Not even the presidential plane escaped his scrutiny. When the president arrived at Bamako after a state visit to the United Arab Emirates, Sacko's customs officials scrupulously searched the baggage of presidential aides and uncovered a large number of luxury goods that the latter had hoped to bring in duty free. Because of his lightning raids and swift and decisive actions against corrupt officials, he was also dubbed "Kamikaze," the nemesis of wealthy businessmen and politicians.

By summer 1987, Sacko was the most popular and most talked-about man in Mali, which, combined with his scrupulous honesty and zeal in ferreting out corruption, made him both a political threat and a danger to the vested interests of businessmen and high government officials. In late August, having learned that 330 pounds of gold were to be registered and shipped as 110 pounds, he attempted to break up an important gold-smuggling network at Bamako's airport. Leading the operation himself, he ordered the plane on which the gold was to be sent searched in order to have it taxed before export. No gold was found, as the exporter had had advance warning of the raid. Sacko then grounded the plane and its crew, an action reversed the following day by Prime Minister Mamadou Dembélé. On August 27, Sacko resigned as minister and was replaced by Mohammed Alhousseyni Touré. Sacko told the press that the reason for his resignation was that he had been "insufficiently supported" in his attempts to expose the gold-smuggling scheme. His enemies in Bamako were glad to see him go, characterizing his anticorruption campaign as out of control. This was a sentiment not shared by most of the rank and file of the government bureaucracy.[11]

In November 1987, the delay in payment of teacher salaries and student stipends led to a boycott of classes at the Ecole Normale Supérieure and the threat of a strike at the Ecole Nationale de l'Administration. Payments were in arrears two months, and the government responded by ordering the payment of salaries and stipends due the previous two weeks. This partial concession did not resolve the problem, which progressively worsened, leading to a three-day teachers' strike in Bamako in early March 1988, which paralyzed all public schools. The strike, called by the Syndicat National de l'Education et de la Culture (SNEC), affected 400,000 schoolchildren and 15,000 teachers. By that time, teachers had not received their salaries for four months. The government tried to head the strike off by hastily convening a meeting with representatives from the union, the federation of unions, and women's organizations. Following its usual policy, the government forcibly transferred 70 teachers to new posts. This in turn gave cause to the students, already disgruntled by the late payment of their stipends. In mid-March, students at the Ecole Normale Supérieure tried to march on the Ministry of Education to protest the transfer of a philosophy lecturer. The demonstration was broken up by the police and the march prevented.

Student and teacher protests had become a regular feature of the political scene in Mali in 1979 and 1980, but were not a determining variable in the country's political course. Their protests did not draw support from other segments of either the civil service or from the employees of parastatals. In fact, many ordinary Malians, themselves affected by delayed salary payments, saw these strikes and demonstrations as examples of a lack of any sense of civic responsibility for the needs of the country as a whole. For despite inefficiency and corruption, the government often lacks the funds to meet its payroll and partly due to that shortfall, has adopted a policy of salary payment delays as part of its economic reform program.

In March 1988, the UDPM held its third regular congress in Bamako, and President Traoré was reelected secretary-general of the party. In a move aimed at revitalizing the party, several members of the powerful Central Executive Bureau (BEC) were replaced, including General Baba Diarra, deputy secretary-general of the BEC and once the vice president of the CMLN. In his addresses to the congress, President Traoré made it clear that the economy was the government's principal concern and that developing countries such as Mali were the victims of what he termed "slow trade exchanges and monetary disorders." He emphasized that the fall in the international price of cotton, Mali's principal export, and debt servicing, particularly that to other states for direct bilateral loans, were jeopardizing Mali's socioeconomic life. These messages made it clear to Malians that most of the country's economic woes were due to forces beyond the government's control.[12] They were also more than a hint to bilateral lenders that loan forgiveness would be welcomed. Prior to the congress, Mali had benefited from the conversion of $413 million in loans into outright grants from the Federal Republic of Germany during the state visit of President Richard von Weizsacker.

During the congress, Traoré also reaffirmed his commitment to the "moralization" campaign. Such a reaffirmation was necessary, given the doubts that had arisen about the government's support for the campaign after the resignation of Finance Minister Soumana Sacko in August 1987.

Prime Minister Mamadou Dembélé, in his address to the congress, recommitted the government to its domestic policy of widening free enterprise and reducing the size and number of parastatals. With regard to the latter, he was quite specific, stating that the government hoped to reduce their number from the current level of forty to fifteen and that ultimately only six would remain.

The government has firmly adhered to its domestic policy of enlarging the free economy and restructuring the public sector, despite the political risks that this has entailed. The restructuring of the public sector has had social costs in part alleviated for the short term by a fund financed by the World Bank for those whose public-sector jobs are redundant. At the 1988 party congress, Prime Minister Mamadou Dembélé stressed that Malians must accept the fact that the state cannot be their only source of employment. This is little comfort to the unemployed and educated youth who, since the adoption of Modibo Keita's socialist options in 1960, always looked to government for employment and who must now seek it in a private sector still in its infancy. During a state visit to the United States in early October 1988, Traoré reaffirmed his government's commitment to expanding the private sector of the economy and encouraging private enterprise.[13] The ability or inability of the private sector to grow and provide employment for young Malians will be a determining factor in the country's politics in the 1990s.

In June 1988, President Traoré again shifted his cabinet and abolished the post of prime minister, two years after its creation. It had become increasingly clear that the position of prime minister was a post in search of functions, as it was without line authority in the government.

Frequent cabinet shuffles, National Assembly elections in which many incumbents are turned out, and regular revitalization of the UDPM in which key politicians lose powerful positions constitute the essentials of democratic process in Mali under President Traoré. They also represent political strategies that prevent many political leaders from building significant power bases through either the electoral process or cabinet-level appointment; most political leaders do not remain in power very long. This has served well the interests of the president, since political challenges to his preeminence are minimized. Meanwhile, the public is kept satisfied to a degree with political processes played out in several arenas, some of which include civilian participation, and those hopeful of ministerial appointment are kept happy. The result is that there are no obvious political heirs who have been groomed to succeed and the president's position is more secure.

Political structures and elections matter more to urban elites than to the rural population. The social and economic welfare of urban elites as well as opportunities in education and employment are all significantly affected by political policies and the political process. For these reasons, the urban elites take an avid interest in elections and have a real sense of political participation in choosing from a roster of several UDPM candidates running for the same position. By comparison, rural subsistence farmers and herdsmen are less concerned about economic and social issues, education, and cash economy employment. Thus, they take less interest in elections and the political process. Ethnicity has not been a factor in Mali's recent elections.

Although President Traoré remains politically preeminent, he has been careful to involve both the UDPM leadership and the National Assembly in key policy matters. This represents an extension of the consensus-building approach that characterized the CMLN. The presence of civilian majorities in the cabinet and in the party leadership in the late 1980s represents significant political accommodation on the part of Traoré and his military supporters.

Traoré's political success rests on the adoption of pragmatic domestic and foreign policies, power sharing with civilians, the use of consensus within the UDPM leadership to formulate policy, regular national and local elections that give the public a limited participatory role in government, substantial external foreign assistance, and a special place for the military in the political life of the country. The support of the army, which Traoré heads, is essential to his continuance as Mali's leader. Military officers occupy some key ministerial posts and positions in the UDPM leadership and are regularly brought into the consensus-building process governing policy formulation. The needs of the military and their families are seen to and special privileges accorded them. Although these measures help to ensure loyalty, they are no guarantee that some junior officers will not try to seize power for themselves, as has happened in the past.

5

Culture and Society

Mali is the heir to a large number of cultural traditions, which in recent decades have been modified by modernization, urbanization, and the gradual conversion of the followers of indigenous religions to Islam. The limited economic opportunities in rural areas have resulted in a rural exodus to the towns and cities and to the job markets of Mali's coastal neighbor, the Ivory Coast. In addition, significant numbers of Sarakole from northwestern Mali have migrated to France in search of work. All of these forces have placed strains on the country's traditional social structures and have caused irreversible changes in the cultural traditions that are closely tied to them. Traditional values have been questioned and even abandoned by many younger Malians who have been exposed to the influences of secular public education. Whereas they and a small cadre of intellectuals strive to move Mali forward as a modern technological state with a place in international cultural circles, other forces are promoting the spread of Islam among animists. Young animist males often find in Islam an escape from the domination of village-based gerontocracies, which, through a complex system of age grades, initiation societies, and land tenure, control capital accumulation. Meanwhile, unemployed youth in the towns and cities often find solace in Islamic orthodoxy, as do older men and women who have been disappointed with their economic fate in life.

ETHNICITY

Race and ethnic attitudes in Mali are often determined by ethnocentric worldviews influenced by religious affiliation. In view of Mali's diverse ethnic groups, it is remarkable that the country has been relatively free from the overt racial and ethnic strife found in so many other areas of Africa. The absence of such strife is in part due to the fact that most ethnic groups are geographically distributed in low-human-density areas and pursue economic activities such as trading, fishing, farming, and pastoralism that do not compete but rather complement those of their neighbors. The inexorable rise in the country's population will place ever-increasing pressures on available arable land and erode traditional divisions of labor, thus increasing the risks for interethnic strife.

The competition for employment in a scarce job market also holds potential for fueling interethnic rivalries. Competition between the Peul and Dogon for mineral wealth lay at the bottom of violent clashes that took place in the Ivory Coast at the mining town of Tortiya in May 1988. A Peul who discovered a rich vein was killed, and his fellows automatically assumed that the Dogon had committed the murder. They attacked the Dogon in retaliation, and in the subsequent violence five people were killed and several injured. Ivorian troops, which had to be called in to break up the ethnic violence, arrested over 100 people.[1] In Mali, the Peul pastoralists currently live in harmony with the Dogon agriculturists, although in the precolonial era they frequently fought. The incident in the Ivory Coast demonstrated how close to the surface are ethnic tensions between them in a modern cash economy setting and how easily they can erupt in violence.

Mutual aid and assistance long ago developed among diverse ethnic groups within the contexts of age sets and clan affiliations and are frequently expressed in a modern context as favoritism in the hiring of personnel for jobs in the bureaucracy. At both the national and the local levels, the government practices this "ethnic patronage." Conscious attempts are made to give representation in high government posts to representatives from all the major ethnic groups. Cabinet ministers inevitably give choice appointments to individuals from their own ethnic group, as do the heads of parastatals, several of which are controlled by specific ethnic groups. For example, the Songhay, from the east of Mali, once controlled the national airline, Air Mali, not to the point of excluding all others from employment, but sufficiently to ensure that only Songhay held key positions. Ethnic patronage, though resented by outsiders, was tolerated because every group successfully practiced it. Conscious of the danger of ethnic politics, however, the government has never tolerated ethnic political associations or ethnic groupings within the party.

Social stratifications within various ethnic groups are the rule and in modern times have led to intraethnic tensions. Among all ethnic groups, individuals are freemen, craftsmen, or serfs/slaves. Although the legal status of the last named was abolished in the early days of colonial rule, social attitudes toward them persist. Among the Bambara and Malinke, craftsmen (*nymankala*) and slaves (*djon*), for example, are viewed as occupying an inferior social status to freemen (*horon*), and intermarriage between the groups is socially unacceptable. Young educated

Peul woman, Mopti (photo by author)

Malians who attempt such cross-caste marriages usually precipitate serious social conflicts within their families. It is interesting that interethnic marriages, though not favored, are frequently acceptable as long as they occur within the same caste.[2]

Smoldering racial attitudes and interethnic class divisions are unlikely to threaten Mali's national unity. Most Malians, especially the young, view their Malian identity as more important than their ethnic one. The mixing of diverse groups in secondary, technical, and post-secondary schools has led to both understanding and tolerance among the educated elites, and the same has occurred in the army, gendarmerie, and the police force.

The Mande speakers, who include the Bambara, Malinke, Marka, and Bozo, comprise half the country's population. Speaking mutually understandable dialects, they dominate the political and economic life of the country. Among the Mande speakers, the Bambara are the most important. In the central and western areas of the country, Bamanankan, the language of the Bambara, has been adopted by many others as a lingua franca. This has in part been facilitated by its long-standing use as the language of trade. The presence of numerous Bambara-speaking government officials in various regions of the country has also served to extend use of the language. The Bambara, who currently number 3.5 million, dominate the social and political life of the country. However, their influence is least in the north and east, where the Songhay, Tuareg, and Maure are found. However, even in these distant regions, "Bambarization" is taking place, albeit in subtle ways.

The Tuareg, Berber nomads who number around 50,000, have been a major source of tension and interethnic conflict. Highly individualistic and distinctly different in both cultural and racial terms from the majority of Malians, they have not found it easy living in a modern black African state. Of the 50,000 Tuareg in Mali, only some 10 percent are pure Berber, the remaining ones being of mixed African heritage. The Tuareg nobles, who consider themselves as nonblack, historically lived in a socially stratified society in which black captives were relegated to serf and slave status. Tuareg race attitudes have little modified because the group has gone to great lengths to preserve its traditional pastoral way of life. In so doing, they have been relatively isolated from the mainstream of Malian life, from education, modernization, and contact with most other groups. Their Berber cultural reference gives them an affinity for Algeria and Libya, and since independence many of them have moved to the former.

Many Malians rationalize their negative feelings and attitudes about the Tuareg on the basis of precolonial exploitation of blacks by the latter. However, these attitudes do not derive solely from events of the past; it is significant that they come from an inability to accommodate a group that is dramatically different in both cultural and racial terms from the majority and that has tenaciously refused to change. In brief, the Tuareg are viewed as unwanted foreigners. These negative attitudes were given a new rationale by the protracted Tuareg revolt of the early 1960s, which cast them as traitors in the popular view.

Early Malian government policies toward the Tuareg did not foster national integration but rather ensured alienation. Many innocent Tuareg were brutalized by the Malian army during the revolt of the 1960s. A number fled to Algeria and Niger, and those who remained behind were frequently harassed by the government. The government's aim was to avert a secessionist movement and to deprive Algeria of a reason for intervention and possible territorial expansion. Reducing the numbers of Tuareg on Malian soil and breaking them as a social entity and political force were seen as means for achieving these ends.[3]

Despite the government's oppressive efforts, the Tuareg remained a significant force in the north. It was finally a succession of two droughts in 1970–1974 and 1984–1985 that dealt the insular Tuareg their greatest blow. During the 1970–1974 drought, the Malian government at first remained indifferent to widespread starvation among the Tuareg. Many outside observers saw this as a crude and inhuman attempt to use famine in order to liquidate a potential political threat. This government strategy eventually failed because some 20,000 Tuareg refugees fled to relief camps in Algeria and Niger and told the international press about the Malian government's failure to help them. International pressure eventually forced the Malians to launch a famine relief effort on behalf of the Tuareg and other northern peoples. Because of the plight of these peripheral populations, Mali became the beneficiary of massive bilateral and international relief aid, which greatly benefited the country as a whole.[4] During the 1984–1985 drought, the government settled Tuareg in various parts of the country and successfully helped some to become farmers. In recent years, a number of dissident Malian Tuareg have sought refuge in Libya, where some have been given military training. It is difficult to ascertain the precise number of Tuareg who have left Mali in recent years because census data for them have been imprecise in the past.

Mali's non-African population has never been significant; it consists primarily of Europeans belonging to diplomatic missions and technical assistance programs. Prior to independence there were several hundred Lebanese in the country, primarily involved in commerce. However, with the rapid development of a state-run economy, most left for neighboring African states. The rapid Africanization of government services at independence led to a decline in the French population, which was never more than a few thousand. Mali has been a refuge for many thousands of Guineans who fled from Sékou Touré's Guinea. These political refugees primarily settled in Bamako.

RELIGION

Islam has gradually won converts in Mali since its introduction with North African traders in the eleventh century A.D. Today, some 65 percent of the people embrace Islam. However, among recent converts, elements of indigenous religions are often retained and syncretic practices are common. Islam is practiced according to the Malikite rite, and most Moslems in the country belong to either of the two major Moslem brotherhoods, the Qadiriya and the Tijaniya. In addition, smaller numbers belong to the Hamalliya. These brotherhoods, or *tariqa*s ("the way" in Arabic), are distinguished by minor differences in rituals and codes of conduct. They are all mystical orders founded by individual mystics and are offensive to orthodox Moslems.

The Qadiriya, which was organized in Baghdad in the eleventh century, was introduced into Mali in the fifteenth century and eventually won many adherents in the eastern part of the country, where it remains strong today. The Tijaniya, founded in Fez, Morocco, in the eighteenth century, was popularized in Mali in the mid- and late nineteenth century by El Hadj Omar Tall. This brotherhood became popular in trading centers and also along the rail line from Senegal. At present, it has many adherents in the western and central part of the country.

An offshoot of the Tijaniya is the Hamalliya, first popularized in western Mali at Nioro around 1900. Prior to the development of political parties in the French Sudan, it had popular appeal among the young because it served as a vehicle for expressing anticolonial sentiments. The members of this order were responsible for a number of violent incidents between 1922 and 1943, which resulted in the eventual exile of their leader, Shaykh Mohammed Al Tishiti Hamallah. In recent years, the Hamalliya has had little appeal to young Malians. At present, the brotherhood's following is fairly small and concentrated in northwestern Mali.[5]

After World War II, a fundamentalist antibrotherhood movement known as the Wahabiya was introduced into the country by pilgrims returning from Saudi Arabia. The followers of this sect are known as the *bras croisés* (crossed arms) because they pray with their arms crossed over their breasts instead of at their sides. Many Wahabi are wealthy merchants and are concentrated in Bamako. In 1957, the Wahabi were the victims of serious riots there that were largely fueled by economic jealousies.[6]

Moslem worshippers leaving the great mosque at Mopti (photo by author)

None of the Islamic brotherhoods or sects has achieved cohesive influence over its followers as they have in neighboring Senegal. However, sect and brotherhood leaders do make their views known to the government and exert a certain degree of political influence. Conscious of the dangers of sectarian politics, the Malian government has repeatedly reaffirmed that the country is laic in nature.

Islam is the predominant religion among the Sarakole, Maure, Tuareg, Songhay, Dioula, and Tukulor. The Bozo, Peul, and Somono are not totally Islamized, but large numbers of them profess to be Moslems. Animism is still strong in the south and west among the Bambara, Malinke, Bobo, Senufo, and Dogon. However, even among these peoples, Islam continues to gain new converts. Syncretic practices continue for many years, but indigenous religions are in gradual retreat.

Islam has received additional impetus from Arab countries, such as Saudi Arabia, Libya, Kuwait, Algeria, and Egypt. Saudi Arabia financed the construction of Bamako's new mosque in the 1970s, whereas other Arab countries have provided cultural and educational assistance in the form of scholarships and programs to foster the learning of Arabic. In 1987, an Islamic Center whose construction was financed by Libya and the United Arab Emirates was opened in Bamako. It consists of a mosque, a library, an auditorium, sixteen classrooms, an administrative building, and a sports center. Both Libya and the United Arab Emirates have pledged to pay for operating for a twenty-five-year period.[7] Arab countries have increasingly become involved in providing Mali with economic aid. In the 1980s, for example, the Arab Bank for Economic Development in Africa provided funds to pave the 360-mile Sévaré-Gao road.

In the late 1980s, there were in Mali approximately 80,000 Christians, of which approximately 80 percent were Catholic. Catholicism was introduced by the White Fathers (the Order of Our Lady of Africa of Algiers) in the western part of the country in the late nineteenth century. By 1895, there were Catholic missions as far east as Timbuctoo. The greatest number of converts has been made among the Bobo people in the *cercles* of San and Tominian, among the Dogon, and in Bamako. There are five dioceses in Mali (Kayes, Mopti, San, Ségou, and Sikasso) and one archdiocese (Bamako). There are some 160 resident priests and 150 nuns, who operate approximately 65 educational institutions as well as dispensaries. In 1972, an agreement between the church and the government integrated the former's schools into public education. The Catholic church in Mali has maintained a strict noninvolvement in political matters.

Protestant missions were first established in Mali in 1918 by the Gospel Missionary Union. The group now has a large number of missions in the central, southern, and western *cercles* of the country from Kita to Ségou. The Christian Missionary Alliance, which arrived in 1923, has been especially active in the southern and east-central *cercles*, extending from Sikasso in the south to Douentza in the east. The Evangelical Baptist Mission has functioned in the area of the Niger Bend at Niafunké, Timbuctoo, and Gao since 1949, while the United World Mission has worked in the extreme west of the country at Kayes and Kenieba since 1952. Since 1961, the various Protestant churches in Mali have been grouped into a federation recognized by the government and are members of the Association of Evangelical Churches of Africa and Madagascar. At present, there are some 90 U.S. missionaries and dependents in Mali and close to 160 Malian pastors. Major bible training schools are maintained at Mana (Bamako), N'Torosso (San), and Kéniéba. Protestant missionaries have made many converts among the Bobo people of Tominian, among the Dogon and Bambara, and in Bamako. Many missions maintain dispensaries and operate dental and maternal and child health clinics.[8]

WOMEN

Mali's traditional societies are primarily patrilineal and patrilocal gerontocracies in which women are relegated to a status below that of men. Many of these societies possess oral traditions consisting of mythologies and legends, elaborated by men, that provide a rationale for the inferior status of women.[9] Conversion to Islam denies men the ability to muster their traditional religious evidence for the inferior status of women. However, they have been adept at representing the status of women in Islam as far inferior to what that religion teaches.

Despite these obstacles, the role and status of women in Malian society are slowly changing. Greater access to education beginning in the 1960s set the stage for easier access to politics and development programs and enabled women to have a stronger voice in society. In 1955, five years prior to independence, the ratio of boys to girls in primary school grades was 3:1; in secondary school it was 10:1. By 1972, the male/female ratio in primary education was 2:1. In secondary education it was 9:1. In 1986, there were only 252 women in the Ecole Nationale d'Administration and 1,491 men.[10] Literacy rates for men are ten times greater than those for women. (The progress in access to education for women in Mali has been far less than in neighboring Senegal.)

Although women were empowered to vote after World War II, none held a major elected political office until the 1980s when three women were elected to the National Assembly. It was not until 1968 that a women, Ina Cissé, was appointed to the cabinet as Secretary of State in the Presidency for Social Affairs. In 1979, Gakou Fatou Niang was appointed minister of information and telecommunications, and in 1986, Sidibé Aissata Cissé was named minister of public health and social affairs.[11] These appointments represented important political gains for women. However, it will be many years before women become a significant force in politics.

The Union Nationale des Femmes Maliennes (UNFM) is a 350,000-member unit within the country's only political party, UDPM. In some respects, the UNFM is akin to the women's auxiliary unit of a male-dominated organization, confined to a set agenda of issues and deprived of equal access to power sharing. This group focuses on women's concerns, has a voice in relevant political issues, but exercises little real power.

Educated women have entered the urban job market as secretaries, clerks, and health workers, whereas their unskilled counterparts often find work in factories and as domestics. Very often, however, neither exert control over their capital accumulation because their salaries are given to their husbands or fathers. Yet, the growing numbers of educated and employed women are slowly challenging male dominance. In urban areas, many women now insist that their husbands opt for a monogamous marriage at the time of their nuptials. This precludes their husbands from marrying a second or third wife. Many educated Malian women view polygamy as a major symbol of sex discrimination. Their husbands frequently see it now as an economic strain they cannot afford and thus freely choose monogamy.

Women play an important role in the health care delivery system, particularly as nurses and midwives. They are heavily concentrated in maternal and child health clinics as well as in family-planning programs. Of interest is the fact that women play an important role in traditional healing among most ethnic groups.[12] Women have also been prominent in a number of agricultural extension programs and in rural literacy programs.

Although women in Bamako have made appreciable gains in their status, their sisters in the countryside are far behind them. There, traditional values reinforced by Islam have kept women in an inferior status and denied them access to education, capital accumulation, and political power. The rural exodus of males to Bamako and to the job markets of the Ivory Coast and France has left many rural women with increased responsibilities and little chance to escape their traditional roles.

YOUTH

Sixty percent of Mali's population is less than twenty years of age. As in most countries, Mali's youth have quickly embraced new ideas and values and are less attached to the traditional values of their elders. Providing jobs for Mali's ever-increasing numbers of young people has been a difficult challenge for the government. Close to 25,000 youth enter the urban job market each year. Many are individuals who have been weeded out of the educational system by competitive examinations and who possess few or limited skills and high expectations with regard to future living standards. In addition, the country's institutions of higher education graduate close to 3,000 individuals, who in years past were guaranteed employment in either the government bureaucracy or in parastatals. With the dismantling of the state-run economy, they must now seek employment in an almost nonexistent private sector. These facts, coupled with the country's stagnant economy, have led to high levels of unemployment.

Students, especially those in secondary and postsecondary schools, are a privileged elite in Mali, although they rarely see themselves as such. Student unrest has already been the most serious political issue that the government has had to face during the 1980s. Most of this unrest has been due to the government's inability to provide stipends and guarantee employment after graduation. The failure of large numbers of graduates to find work in either the government or the private sector will lead to more unrest and threaten the stability of the government.

Street crime in Bamako has become a serious problem, whereas in the 1960s it was virtually nonexistent. In large measure, street crime is committed by unemployed youth who find no acceptable alternative. Islamic leaders blame this development on modernization and the rejection of religious values and morals. Others make the government the scapegoat; they accuse officials of corruption and greed and claim those problems create unemployment. The government, sensitive to these accusations, established an anticorruption campaign in 1986 after the UDPM adopted its anticorruption charter.

Rural youth find a solution to their dilemma by migrating to the capital or to job markets in the Ivory Coast or France. Often this migration is seasonal, with young men returning at the beginning of the planting season in May and leaving after the harvest in October. In recent years, many Malians have migrated to France, where 25,000–30,000 work as unskilled laborers, janitors, and in other menial jobs. A large proportion are Sarakole from the Kayes region in the west of the country.[13] Undocumented Malian migrants have increasingly created problems for French authorities, and in October 1987, 101 of them were forcibly returned to Mali, creating diplomatic strains between the two countries. Most migrants live in crowded conditions in French cities, where they are vulnerable to diseases such as tuberculosis, which has for some years been a major problem among these migrants.

Migrants who return to Mali do so with new ideas and values, less attachment to traditional values, and a degree of earned independence from traditional village authorities. There is little family resistance to their migrations, as their earnings help support those left behind. Those who return often serve as innovators of change in rural areas because of their newly acquired values and ideas; they are more receptive to improved agricultural technologies. In an effort to stem migration, several programs have been directed at assisting young rural farmers to remain on the land.[14]

Mali's current birthrate, the nature of its economy, and limited employment opportunities spell major difficulties in the future for the government. For if the government is unable to find employment for urban youth and improve the lot of rural peasants, it will be faced with growing frustration and anger capable of threatening the country's political stability.

EDUCATION

Mali's current educational system consists of nine years of basic education, the completion of which provides students with a Diplôme des Etudes Fondamentales (DEF). After grade 6, students are given an examination and if they pass, receive a diploma for primary education. High failure rates at both points, after grades 6 and 9, limit the numbers who progress to the next level and contribute to the large numbers of unemployed youth. Grades 10 to 12 constitute the lycée, after which a secondary-level baccalaureate is given to those who pass a stiff examination. Students can then go on to a variety of postsecondary training colleges that usually have four-year courses of study. These schools, which are not considered university level, include the Ecole Nationale d'Administration (1,743 students), the Ecole Nationale d'Ingénieurs (470 students), the Ecole Nationale de Médecine et de Pharmacie (300 students), the Ecole Normale Supérieure (1,760 students), the Institut Polytechnique Rural de Katibougou (2,000 students), and the Institut Supérieur de Formation et Recherche Appliquée. There are variations in the duration of the courses of study, medicine and pharmacy being six years, whereas those as Katibougou's polytechnical institute vary from four to seven years.

Even before independence, Malians had to go abroad for university-level education. Since independence, the majority—a few thousand—have obtained university-level training in the Eastern bloc countries, particularly, the Soviet Union, Poland, Romania, Bulgaria, and Czechoslovakia. A slightly smaller number have studied in France and fewer than a hundred in the United States. Study in Eastern bloc universities is facilitated by grants from host countries that cover travel, tuition, and living expenses. Malians are anxious to obtain university-level education and have avidly competed for these grants. The Eastern bloc countries are motivated by the prospect of influencing the future educated elites and of indoctrinating them in the principles of Marxism-Leninism. In many cases, so much time is given over to studying Marxism that returning Malian students complain bitterly that their exposure to their main field of study is curtailed.

Degrees, diplomas, certificates, and courses of study in the Eastern bloc are now perceived by many Malians as being of inferior quality. This is based on experience with returnees, many of whom have had to be retrained either in France or in Dakar. For example, physicians and dentists returning from training in Poland and the Soviet Union in the 1970s were found to be seriously deficient in both their knowledge of basic medical science and in clinical skills. They had to be sent for a year of further training to the Faculty of Medicine at the University of Dakar.[15] Although many young Malians now would prefer university training in the West, the absence of financial aid to cover travel, tuition, and living costs often gives them no other option but to go to universities in the Eastern bloc.

During the 1980s, there were in Mali some 1,558 primary schools, with 364,382 students. There were 20 secondary schools, with 13,227 students, indicating that fewer than 4 percent of primary-school students moved on to secondary education. In 1989, 95.4 percent of the adult population over age 25 had no formal education, 4 percent had attained a primary educational level, and 0.6 percent a secondary level. Literacy among males over age 15 was 18.6 percent; for females it was 1.8 percent. Mali has had an extensive adult literacy program in operation since the late 1960s. It has achieved significant success in both rural and urban areas.

Although universal primary education is guaranteed to all Malians, the educational system is incapable of accommodating all who deserve to move on to higher levels. The DEF examination is exceedingly difficult and structured, more to limit access than to assess ability. Large numbers of literate semieducated and unemployed youth now crowd Mali's capital, Bamako, where they represent a disaffected group, and many of them resort to crime and become politically radicalized.

Koranic education is widespread in Mali, being conducted by marabouts (Islamic teachers and spiritual leaders) in their courtyards or in a more formalized manner in *medersas*, which are religious schools usually attached to mosques. Most of those exposed to this type of education are very young children, who learn to memorize and recite passages from the Koran and to write them with ink in Arabic, often on wooden boards. The boards are washed with water and then reused. Children do not learn Arabic in most of these schools and have no idea of the meaning of Arabic words. This type of Koranic education is often ended once children enter primary school.

Advanced Islamic education is provided at the Lycée Franco-Arab in Timbuctoo and at some schools in Bamako. However, the number of students attending these schools is few. Those wishing to go on to advanced levels of Islamic religious education usually study individually under noted local marabouts. Some travel to Senegal and elsewhere in search of such education, and a few to go Egypt and Saudi Arabia. The Islamic Center opened in 1987 in Bamako offers both introductory and advanced religious Islamic instruction and thus has an appreciable impact on Islamic education in Mali.

Religious education for Roman Catholics and Protestants is conducted through the respective churches. Indigenous Protestant clergy are trained in Mali at Mana, to the south of Bamako, at Kéniéba, and at N'Torosso. During the 1970s and 1980s, a large number of Malian clergy were trained at this facility. Catholic Malians wishing to enter the priesthood must travel out of the country for advanced training.

Bambara blacksmiths sculpting statues, Sarro (photo by author)

THE ARTS AND POPULAR CULTURE

The traditional representational art forms of the Bambara and Dogon people of Mali are well known, and examples of them are found in museums all over the world. These art forms are closely linked to traditional values and religious beliefs, which have been in steady decline for several decades. Islam, which has made substantial progress, is intolerant of representational art, and not surprisingly these art traditions have declined as Islamic orthodoxy has increased. In an attempt to preserve ancient artistic traditions and to adapt them to the modern world, the French established the Maison des Artisans in 1932; in 1966 it became the Institut National des Arts. Few traditional masks and other sculptures in wood and iron are still being made for ritual use. However, modern Malian sculptors, many of whom are trained at the institute, have proven their skills in producing modern works that draw upon the past. There is a national museum (Musée Nationale) in Bamako that contains collections of Mali's traditional arts. A regional branch museum was opened in Gao in the early 1980s with the assistance of the Ubersee Museum of Bremen, West Germany.

Traditional weaving of colorful blankets, covers, and cloths continues among all of Mali's major ethnic groups. Likewise, traditional leather working and jewelry making are also widely practiced.

Dogon ancestor shrine, Lower Ogol (photo by author)

Mali established a national dance group in 1959 and a national theater group in 1969. Both groups have performed throughout the world and have been the recipients of numerous distinctions and awards. The national dance troupe, although performing a number of recently choreographed dances, also performs many traditional ones using masks.

Mali has a rich musical heritage handed down through generations of *dyeliu* (bards), who are also oral historians and praise singers. Playing guitars and the kora (a twenty-one-string lute), a number of these traditional bards have achieved widespread recognition outside of Mali. They include kora musicians such as Sidiki Diabaté and Batrou Sékou Kouyaté, and the blind guitarist Bassoumana Cissoko, who died in 1988 at the age of 97. Cissoko's songs were used for many years as signature tunes for Radio Mali and to mark important events such as the 1968 coup d'état.

In the early 1960s, most instrumentalists were members of the National Instrumental Ensemble, a group whose songs often carried the political messages of the Keita government. The group toured Africa and Europe, including the Soviet Union, and won the gold medal at the Pan-African Cultural Festival in Algiers in 1966. Although leading vocalists and instrumentalists continued to participate in the national ensemble after the 1968 coup d'état, they were given considerable freedom to play on their own. A number of younger talented musicians have never belonged to the National Instrumental Ensemble. Because most traditional instrumentalists are also bards, they have served as praise singers for political leaders. Other nonmusician *dyeliu* such as Garanké Mamou Sylla, who died in 1988, translated the speeches of both presidents Keita and Traoré into local languages whenever they toured rural areas. Today, *dyeliu* continue to function as praise singers for individual patrons, be they politicians or people who engage them for specific social events.

In 1970, the Malian Ministry of Information, in conjunction with Musicaphon of the Federal Republic of Germany, issued the first anthology of Malian music as an album of six 33 RPM records. Most of Mali's major musical artists were recorded in this series, including the leading kora musicians, Sidiki Diabaté, Batrou Sékou Kouyaté, and Djelimadi Sissoko. Also represented were the leading vocalists of the time, Fanta Damba, Nantenedie Kamissoko, Wande Kouyaté, Mogontafé Sacko, Tata Kouyaté, and Saranfing Kouyaté, as well as the leading xylophone players, Brahima Kouyaté and Loutigui Diabaté, and the guitarist Solo Diabaté. In 1971, the Ministry of Information, in conjunction with Musicaphon, issued two recordings by the guitarist Bassoumana Cissoko: "The Old Lion I" and "The Old Lion II." The release of these recordings was a major breakthrough for traditional Malian music and helped set the stage for a later generation of younger musicians who would produce their own recordings in Europe.

The traditional musicians have long enjoyed successful European, U.S., and Asian tours. Their melodies and lyrics still have great appeal to non-Malian audiences, as evidenced by the successful European tour in 1986 of the guitarist Ousmane Sacko, and his vocalist wife, Yiakare Diabaté, who also produced a popular recording at the same time. Younger musicians have adapted traditional rhythms and melodies to electric instruments. These include Zani Diabaté and Super Djata, who have each toured Europe several times and produced popular recordings. Both of these artists are extremely popular and have large followings in Africa, Europe, and the United States.

Mali's most popular male vocalist in the late 1980s has been Salif Keita, whose compelling voice and wailing singing style has made him a superstar in both Africa and Europe. He has produced a number of albums and tapes in Europe, including "Mandjou" (1979), "Wale" and "Primprin" (1981), "Djougouya" (1982), "Tounkan" (1983), and "Soro" (1988). Keita's talent has served not only to demonstrate the richness of Mali's music but also to break down the barriers of caste and attitude in Mali. Keita is an albino, a group still disparaged and feared by many in Mali and one once ritually disposed of. He is also not a *dyeli* by birth, and his musical success represents an important break with Mali's past traditions in which only *dyeliu* could be singers.[16] Keita's band, Les Ambassadeurs Internationaux (formerly known as Les Ambassadeurs),

Bambara masked Tyi Wara dancers, Boussin (photo by author)

now uses synthesizers and electric guitars in place of the kora and xylophone. His lyrics consist of anecdotes that deal with current Malian social problems. In spring 1988, Keita made his debut in the United States at the Beacon Theater in New York during the New York International Festival of the Arts.[17]

Mali has produced a number of eminent writers and poets. Prior to independence, a number of Sudanese achieved distinction for their historical and anthropological studies and their collections of legends and proverbs. Among these are Moussa Travélé (*Proverbes et contes Bambara*, 1923), who while serving as an interpreter for the French, also conducted several anthropological studies. Ibrahima Mamadou Ouane (*Le collier de coquillages*, 1957), has also written historical works and works on Islamic jurisprudence. Amadou Hampaté Ba, a distinguished historian, diplomatist, and writer, has produced a number of historical works and fiction such as *L'Etrange destin de Wangrin* (1973). The late Massa Makan Diabaté wrote a number of works based on oral traditions. They include *Si le feu s'éteignait* (1967), *Kala Jata* (1970), *Janjon et autres chants populaires du Mali* (1970), and *L'aigle et l'épervier* (1975). Fily Dabo Sissoko, who, in addition to being a politician, was also a poet, wrote *Poèmes d'Afrique noire* (1963).

Other writers include Bokar N'Diaye (*Veillées au Mali*), Issa Traoré (*Contes et récits du terroir*), Hadj Sadia Traoré (*A l'écoute des gens du village*), Mamadou Gologo (*Mon coeur est un volcan*), and Seydou Badian Kouyaté (*Sous l'orage, Le sang des masques*, and *Noces sacrées*). Gologo and Kouyaté were also prominent politicians and members of the Keita government. Another former political leader, Yoro Diakité, who collaborated with Moussa Traoré in ousting Modibo Keita, wrote a novel, *Une main amie* (1969), which achieved much popularity in Mali. Recent novels from Malian authors include *Le prix de l'âme* (1981) by Moussa Konaté and *Tchagoua né un défunt* (1980) by Nagognime Dembélé.[18]

The best-known Malian novel is *Le devoir de violence* (1968) by Yambo Ouologuem, published in English in 1971 as *Bound to Violence*. This novel, which was widely acclaimed at the time as representing a unique African style of writing, received the Prix Renaudot, a coveted French literary award, in 1968. Ouologuem was the first African writer to be the recipient of such an award. The critical acclaim accorded to both the French and English versions of this book was later significantly tarnished when a number of literary experts noticed major similarities between passages in it and passages from André Schwarz-Bart's *Le dernier des justes* (1969), Graham Greene's *It's a Battlefield* (1934), and passages by other writers.[19]

At independence there was one territorial newspaper, *Le Soudan Français*. This was replaced with a daily, *L'Essor*, a government-controlled publication that actually had begun publication in 1949 and had soon become the official organ of the US-RDA political party. Between 1968 and 1979, the paper was the official publication of the Military Committee of National Liberation, and since 1979 of the UDPM. *L'Essor*, which began with a modest circulation of 2,000, now has a circulation of 4,000. It consists of several pages primarily of local news, including political events, as well as international news, feature stories, and sports. For much of its publication history, *L'Essor* has regularly printed dispatches and stories that have an anti-Western slant, received from Communist news agencies. However, this has changed appreciably in recent years. *Kibaru* is a monthly newspaper, with a 5,000 circulation, published in Bambara and three other languages. Other monthly newspapers are *Barakéla*, the publication of the Union Nationale des Travailleurs du Mali, and *Sunjata*, with a circulation of 3,000, and covering social, economic, and political affairs. Regularly published magazines include *L'Informateur*, a monthly review put out by the Ministry of Information and Telecommunications, *Etudes Maliennes*, a cultural journal published quarterly by the Institut des Sciences Humaines, and *Jamana*, a cultural quarterly. Other publications include *Podium*, a weekly devoted to culture and sports, and the *Journal Officiel de la République du Mali*, produced by the government printers and containing all official notices, regulations, and laws.

There are currently two book publishers in Mali, Librairie Populaire du Mali and Editions-Imprimeries du Mali. The former, which is a parastatal agency, publishes books under the imprint Editions Populaires. Plans were made in the late 1980s to turn over the Librairie Populaire to private hands. The Agence Malienne de Presse et de Publicité (AMPA) is the official government news agency and is under the Ministry of Information and Telecommunications.

In the late 1980s, there were close to 120,000 radio receivers in Mali. In 1983, a national color television network was inaugurated, built with financial aid from Libya. Radio Mali and the television network were later merged into Radiodiffusion-Télévision Malienne. This state agency televises a few hours a day and broadcasts programs over the radio from early morning to late evening. Radio Mali carries news, interviews and discussions, musical entertainment, and dramatic presentations. Most broadcasting is in French, with local language segments regularly aired during the day. In the early 1970s, the People's Republic of China (PRC) constructed a modern radio broadcasting facility on the saddle of the mountain connecting Point-G with Kati. Its antennas have the capacity to reach most of West Africa. In the late 1980s, efforts were made to set up regional radio broadcasting centers around the country.

Both television and radio news in Mali remain heavily local and regional, with major international events only occasionally covered in depth.

The first film made by Malians was *Bambo,* a short fictional feature produced in 1968 by students in Bamako under the direction of a French professor, Georges Legrand. The Service Cinématographique du Ministère de l'Information du Mali (SCINOFMA), the official film production company, has produced a number of films, including *Le retour de Tiéman, Cinq jours d'une vie,* and *Le Mali: carrefour de civilisations.* Several Malian filmmakers have achieved worldwide recognition. They include Moussa Bathily (*La foire internationale de Dakar, Ndakarou, Tiyabu Biru*), Séga Coulibaly (*Le destin*), Alkaly Kaba (*Les Wandyalankas, Walanda-Wanda*), and Djibril Kouyaté (*Le retour de Tiéman*). The most acclaimed Malian filmmaker is Souleymane Cissé. After studying filmmaking in the Soviet Union in the 1960s, he produced several highly regarded films, which include *Den Muso* (1975), *Baara* (1978), *Finyé* (1982), and *Yeelen* (1987). *Finyé* (The wind) depicts student opposition to the regime of Moussa Traoré. Cissé's film *Yeelen* received a jury prize at the Cannes Film Festival in 1987. By the late 1980s, Cissé was among Africa's most acclaimed filmmakers.[20]

Although Malian filmmaking has achieved notable successes, most films shown in movie houses in Mali are produced in either the West or in Communist bloc countries. All films shown in Mali must pass through a panel of censors under the direction of the Ministry of Information.

The most popular sport in Mali is soccer, which was introduced shortly after World War I. It is especially popular with urban youth, and in Bamako the Stade Omnisport, with a capacity of 25,000, is frequently filled to capacity for important matches. Salif Keita (not the vocalist of the same name) is a champion soccer player who has achieved international recognition. Other sports such as basketball, boxing, handball, swimming, judo, and cycling are also popular. Soccer matches with teams from other African countries are often highly charged, emotional events, not the least because the matches serve as surrogates for a number of economic, political, and racial rivalries.

In October 1988, President Moussa Traoré used the tenth biennial meeting of youth, arts, culture, and sports in Bamako to exhort Mali's youth to apply themselves to the discovery of the rich culture of Africa. The meeting, which was attended by 2,000 Malian youths, was the occasion for young people from Mali's seven regions to present plays, ballets, concerts, traditional dances, art exhibitions, and sports shows. Such regular meetings underscore the government's awareness of the country's rich cultural and artistic heritage and reflect its desire to preserve and develop it.[21]

HEALTH AND HEALTH SERVICES

The major disease problems in Mali are nutritional deficiencies and communicable diseases such as bacterial and protozoal dysenteries, malaria, measles, tuberculosis, hepatitis-A and hepatitis-B, onchocerciasis (river blindness), and trypanosomiasis (sleeping sickness). The latter are vector-borne diseases, whose incidence is greatest in the southern and western portions of the country. In recent years, the infant mortality rate in Mali has been on the order of 200/1,000 compared to 17/1,000 for the United States.[22] Most deaths occur in children less than two years of age.

High mortality rates are observed in Mali in children who contract measles and dysentery, as these diseases often occur on top of chronic malaria and other parasitic infections. In addition, many children are either marginally nourished or malnourished and as a consequence not able to produce effective defenses against these diseases. In urban centers, Western patterns of morbidity and mortality are slowly emerging among adults as modern lifestyles and diets are assumed. Chronic hepatitis-B infection and resulting carcinoma of the liver is a major cause of mortality in adults.

Between 1985 and December 1988, close to one hundred cases of Acquired Immunodeficiency Syndrome (AIDS) were diagnosed in Mali, most in the city of Bamako. Many cases of AIDS in Mali, as in other African countries, go undiagnosed. Therefore, the actual number of cases that occurred in this period is probably much higher. Serologic surveys conducted in 1988 among several thousand people in both Bamako and rural areas revealed a pattern of positivity for the Human Immunodeficiency Virus (HIV), the causative agent of AIDS, similar to that previously found in other African countries. Thirty percent of prostitutes tested positive. Among prisoners the rate was 7.8 percent and among blood donors, 0.2 percent. HIV positivity is highest among prostitutes and sexually active young adults in urban areas. It is lowest in rural areas.

Individuals who are HIV positive may not develop clinical AIDS for many years. Thus current rates of HIV positivity are fairly good predictors of the future incidence of the disease. Given current rates of HIV positivity, significant numbers of AIDS cases will occur in Mali throughout the 1990s. In order to monitor HIV positivity rates, the Malian Ministry of Health has undertaken a program of periodic screening.

In December 1988, Mali requested the assistance of the World Health Organization in evaluating and restructuring its AIDS prevention program, which had been in place for a few years. Some of the initiatives of this restructured program include increased public health education, the careful sterilization of all injection equipment (needles and syringes) at all health care facilities and the screening of blood donors for HIV positivity. The Central Biologic Laboratory in Bamako now has the technical capability to routinely perform screening tests for HIV.

The greatest impact on reducing morbidity and mortality rates in Mali has come from public health programs aimed at immunizing the population and improving environmental sanitation. Since independence in 1960, Mali has launched a number of public health programs that have been highly successful. Prominent among these was the Smallpox Eradication–Measles Control Program between 1966 and 1972, which was funded at a cost of $1.2 million by the U.S. Agency for International Development (USAID). During the 1970s, a regional onchocerciasis-control program, coordinated by the World Health Organization (WHO), resulted in the virtual rupture of transmission of the disease in southern Mali.[23] Immunization programs against tuberculosis, yellow fever, meningococcal meningitis[24] and cholera have been regularly implemented with foreign assistance through Mali's Endemic Disease Service. During the late 1980s, special efforts were made to interrupt the transmission of dracunculiasis (Guinea worm) infection in the Mopti region.

Since the early 1970s, Mali has suffered two severe droughts. The first (1970–1974) primarily affected the nomadic populations in the northern part of the country, resulting in famine there. The second (1984–1985) affected the entire country. In early 1974, there were 80,000 famine refugees in some thirty camps in Mali.[25] It is estimated that 20,000 Malians fled to adjacent countries during the drought. Livestock losses during the 1970–1974 drought were on the order of 50 percent in the affected regions. It is estimated that 100,000 people died in the six-country Sahel area during the 1970–1974 drought. Multilateral food aid, much of it from the United States, greatly alleviated the 1974 famine and prevented famine from occurring in 1984–1985.

Health services were first established in the 1890s, primarily by French military physicians.[26] As the colonial government expanded, these physicians also provided services to the indigenous population. It was apparent to these medical officers that health services had to become mobile and stress the prevention of disease if they were to have an appreciable impact on the health of the population. For this reason, and to deal with trypanosomiasis, a mobile medical service was established in French West Africa in 1939. In Mali, this service is called the Service National des Grandes Endémies, "Endemic Disease Service." It conducts mass immunization programs and provides diagnosis and treatment for leprosy, trypanosomiasis, malaria, trachoma, tuberculosis, and other communicable diseases.

Health services were quickly Africanized in Mali in 1960 at independence, in contrast to some neighboring states that maintained closer ties with France. During the 1960s, large numbers of medical and paramedical personnel came from the Soviet Union, North Vietnam, and the People's Republic of China. Malians were sent to study medicine in the Soviet Union, Poland, and the German Democratic Republic. Most of the Malians who went to study medicine in France (about 100 persons) did not return.

The colonial government also established the Assistance Medicale, the curative-care system, which has been greatly expanded since independence. The medical care infrastructure for the late 1980s included 2 national hospitals (Point-G and Gabriel Touré), a regional ophthalmologic hospital administered by the Organisation de Coordination et de Coopération pour la Lutte contre les Grandes Endémies (OCCGE), and 9 regional- and cercle-level hospitals. In principle, each of the 46 cercles and 281 arrondissements have health centers. However, in 1981, some 35 arrondissements did not have such centers. There are 37 private dispensaries, primarily in the regions of Kayes and Sikasso, and private groups also operate 9 maternal and child health clinics.

In 1987, there were a total of 345 health facilities of all kinds in Mali, with 3,543 health personnel. Over half of the health personnel, as well as drugs and supplies, are in the capital, Bamako, and serve 8 percent of the total national population. The Ministry of Health's budget was only 8 percent of the national budget and fell to 4.8 percent in 1980. Yet most health facilities are operated by the government and most personnel are government employees. In general, facilities are poorly maintained, suffer equipment breakdown, and frequently, unless supported by outside donor projects, lack basic supplies and medications. Rises in personnel costs have been met by decreasing the money allocated for drugs and supplies. Thus, many facilities are only marginally functional.

Mali's medical and pharmacy school opened in the early 1970s with French subsidies, is poorly equipped, and often lacks laboratory equipment and supplies. The quality of teaching at the school has greatly improved over the years. However, graduates possess a level of training and competence well below that of graduates of most European and U.S. medical schools. During the late 1970s, it became clear that Mali's state-operated medical care system could not absorb all of the graduates of not only the school of medicine and pharmacy but also those of the nursing school. Since 1985, medicine has no longer been a monopoly service of the state and its constituent institutions. The government's policy of privatizing the economy includes permitting the private practice of medicine and the establishment of private clinics. This, in effect, has absolved the government from providing guaranteed employment to every graduate of health-related schools.

All government employees in Mali are insured for medical care by the ministries for which they work. The ministry does not actually pay, but the employee is in principle covered for 80 percent of the expenses incurred. Some 55,000 salaried workers in Mali are covered by the National Social Welfare Institute, which is a retirement fund, accident fund, family welfare fund, and health insurance fund. An employer contributes a sum equal to roughly 2 percent of an employee's salary for health insurance and 2.4 percent for accidents and retirements. Employees match this with a 1.6 percent contribution. The institute provides medical care through a network of medical centers and dispensaries, 65 percent of whose personnel are in Bamako.[27]

In December 1983, President Traoré signed a decree aimed at cost recovery for medical care, primarily at the two national hospitals, Gabriel Touré and Point-G. A pilot study was carried out at the former in 1984–1985; by 1986, cost-recovery programs were in effect at these two hospitals and at the hospital in Kita. The aim of this cost-recovery program is to make these hospitals capable of generating enough funds to cover most recurrent costs such as medications, equipment, and maintenance. The Malians do not see personnel costs as recurrent ones.[28]

In 1987, the results of the 1986 cost-recovery efforts were published and showed marked differences between the three hospitals; Point-G (7.5 percent); Gabriel Touré (14.9 percent); and Kita (27.1 percent).[29] Point-G Hospital recovers costs by charging from 375 CFA francs to 2,500 CFA francs per day for inpatient care. Outpatient charges at this hospital are 500 CFA per visit. The hospitals do not provide the poor with food, medications, surgical supplies, and laundry, thus passing on these expenses to patients and their families.

The growth of a major private sector in medicine and the ability of government hospitals to recoup major portions of their recurrent costs will be precluded in the near future by the enormous numbers of poor people in Mali, their inability to pay for much of their medical care, and the pervasive attitude that government must do its share in this area. In addition, with shortages of medications common, Malians see little use in paying a user fee to a care giver when the medications prescribed are unavailable. The causes of this longstanding problem lie in the lack of hard currency reserves for purchasing drugs overseas and the absence of a local pharmaceutical industry. Not surprisingly, drug shortages have induced many Malians, particularly those in rural areas where these shortages are worst, to rely on indigenous herbal medications and to consult traditional medical practitioners.

TRADITIONAL MEDICAL CARE

Because Mali has a variety of ethnic groups and cultures, traditional medicine is not a homogeneous system. The many traditional systems have internal pluralism and no formal organization, and the number of traditional practitioners is unknown.

Essentially, traditional medicine assumes natural causes for disease or supernatural causes, such as spirits, ghosts, witchcraft, and sorcery. Practitioners who deal with illness often specialize not only on the basis of the disease but also according to the supposed cause. There is both cooperation and rivalry in relations between practitioners within any category and in relations of practitioners in different categories. It is believed that some practitioners control supernatural causes of disease; thus, they function in both a benevolent and a malevolent manner. Different types of practitioners often have overlapping functions. In Bambara country, for example, one finds high levels of friction between oracle-spirit mediums and diviners and Moslem Koranic teachers. The latter are gradually eroding the client base of the former two in areas where conversion to Islam is taking place.

Use of traditional practitioners is strongly governed by educational status. In cities and towns, where people with higher levels of education are concentrated, there is far less use of traditional practitioners than in rural areas.[30] In addition, the concentration of medical care resources in urban areas and the greater availability of modern drugs there tend to reduce reliance on traditional practitioners.

Modern medicine in rural areas is very often nothing more than a small dispensary and a nurse who has only a few aspirin and antimalarial drugs. This fact is important because the rural population sees modern medicine in this light and unfavorably compares it to local traditional systems. In urban areas, however, because of manpower and resource concentrations, modern medicine has had a major impact in reducing morbidity and mortality.

6

The Economy

When Mali became independent in 1960, its leaders had high hopes for its economy. Almost thirty years later, those hopes have not been met. The country's early political leaders thought that a brighter economic future could be assured through a planned, state-run economy, the issuance of a national currency, a diversification in agriculture, industrialization, and an eventual lessening of dependence on external subsidies and loans. Instead, although Mali has made some progress in agriculture and the development of light industries, real per capita incomes have declined since independence and the country is more than ever heavily dependent on external subsidies, grants, and loans. Severe droughts in the 1970s and 1980s, coupled with fixed producer prices for crops, have stymied agricultural gains, and industrial development has been set back because of rapid rises in oil prices and because the country is both energy and mineral poor. Compounding matters are an excessively bloated state bureaucracy and parastatals, undercapitalization of a number of industries, limited markets for goods and services produced, and widespread corruption.

This litany of economic ills is not unique to Mali. However, it demonstrates the enormous obstacles that countries like Mali must overcome in order to raise themselves out of dependency and underdevelopment. Mali's economic prospects are extremely bleak, certainly in the short term, and probably in the long term as well.

THE PRECOLONIAL AND COLONIAL ECONOMIES

Mali is essentially an agricultural country in which subsistence agriculture has dominated life for countless centuries. Millet, sorghum, and other grains have long been the mainstays of agricultural life; rice, cotton, and peanuts were added later on. During the centuries before the colonial era, a brisk trade flourished in Mali, linking it to the markets of North Africa and later to the European trading posts along the West

African coast. Gold, slaves, civet, and ivory were taken out through entrepôts like Djénné and Timbuctoo, and within the region, local trading networks distributed both agricultural products and manufactures brought in from outside.

French traders first entered the Sudan because of their interest in gum arabic. This substance consists of the dried sap of a number of species of acacia trees and was widely used until recently for manufacturing glues, thickening ink, fixing dye, stiffening cloth, and making candy. When they arrived in the 1850s and 1860s, the French traders found extensive local trading systems. Working out of trading houses already established in St. Louis in Senegal on the coast, they journeyed up the Senegal River in search of gum, which was widely available in the region, and also gathered ivory and shea butter.

French gum traders and their commercial interests in what is now western Mali set the stage for gradual French penetration into the region. African traders under this colonial system were limited to the internal distribution of European manufactures procured from French trading houses and the distribution and sale of local products. Very few African traders were able to break into this French-controlled monopoly, not the least because they were unable to deposit the required capital funds of 10 million French francs necessary for obtaining trading licenses. Two of the most prominent St. Louis–based trading companies were Maurel et Prom, established in 1862, and Etablissements Peyrissac, founded in 1872.

By 1900, in Kayes in the western part of the territory there were thirty-seven trading houses, which were agencies of parent companies in St. Louis. Although their initial activities were limited to the export of gum, the French later diversified as the territory's agricultural resources were developed. For example Peyrissac, which initially concentrated on the gum trade, had quickly turned to peanuts and peanut oil and built a peanut oil refinery in St. Louis in 1881. By 1908, the value of exported peanut products from the Sudan was double that of gum arabic.[1]

The peace created by French colonial rule permitted the spread of indigenous commerce through the establishment of long-distance trading routes, local markets, and weekly fairs. The latter were initiated by the colonial government as a means of assuring the distribution of imported European manufactures. However, they also permitted local populations to come together to barter their agricultural products. The Dioula became prominent in this indigenous commerce and traded in kola nuts, which they brought from the Ivory Coast on the backs of donkeys. They also aided the French trading houses, as they held the key to the redistribution and retail systems.

Until 1920, cowrie shells were used as money in some areas such as Djénné, but barter was the rule. Bank notes were first issued that year and soon became widely used. Coins had been in circulation for several years. During World War I, a number of Lebanese merchants arrived in the colony to fill the vacuum left by French traders who had left to join the armed forces. The colonial administration attempted to create disincentives for the Lebanese but enjoyed little success. They eventually became a prominent commercial force not only in Mali but also in many West African territories. Most of them left Mali shortly after independence because the state-run economy effectively stifled their commercial activities.

Prior to 1923, the town of Kayes dominated the commercial life of the territory. However, with the completion of the railway between Dakar on the coast and Bamako in 1923, the latter became the commercial center. Between the two world wars, a number of large trading companies moved into the territory.[2] Among these were Société Commerciale de l'Ouest Africain (SCOA), Niger Français of Liverpool, Vezia of Bordeaux, and others. Just prior to independence in 1960, commerce in the Sudan was characterized by an almost exclusive monopoly of the French trading companies on imports and exports. Of all the imports, a third were sold directly by the trading companies through their retail outlets and the remainder to some 10,000 licensed African traders. There were some 150 Lebanese traders and a few Europeans functioning at the retail-distribution level of African merchants. Some of them were so successful in amassing capital that they were eventually able to secure import permits and compete with the large firms.

Prior to independence, the Sudan functioned with a balanced budget and an annual income surplus. These facts are somewhat deceiving because sizable subsidies were given to the territory from the richer coastal territories through the federal budget of French West Africa. In addition, the metropole poured in large amounts in direct subsidies after World War II, not only for capital improvements, but also for operations. As early as 1932, in the dead delta of the Niger River, the French created a giant irrigation scheme that was enlarged and improved over the years with the construction of a dam across the Niger River at Markala and the digging of canals. The principal purpose of the scheme, known as the Office du Niger, was cotton production. By 1949, some 44,500 hectares were being irrigated. From its initiation, the project was controversial because of skepticism about its possible productivity and because large numbers of Africans were forced to work on its construction and others forcibly settled in it or else evicted.[3] The Office du Niger prominently figured in French subsidies to the Sudan, consuming 30 percent of them prior to World War II.

French subsidies for the Sudan created two major problems for independent Mali: first, the illusion that the country had been financially sound; and second, a large cadre of wage-earning civil servants living in an artificially supported consumer economy. These politically pivotal civil servants had a relatively high standard of living, compared to that of rural peasants, which was made possible by colonial subsidization. In 1960, their salaries accounted for 60 percent of Mali's national budget. These problems, which loomed large at independence in 1960, are still present, and subsidies, grants, and loans have been consistently used to deal with them.

Most wage earners currently work for the government, either in the civil service or in the parastatals. During the 1980s, under pressure from the International Monetary Fund, the World Bank, and other donors, Mali made efforts both to limit the numbers annually entering government service and to curtail their subsidies. These subsidies include artificially low retail prices for food produced in country, relatively early retirement on good pensions, generous sick and annual leave, free health care and educational benefits for dependents. Reducing these benefits and subsidies has proven difficult and politically hazardous since they have long been seen by beneficiaries as entitlements.

THE CURRENT ECONOMY

Mali's economy is largely based on traditional agriculture, livestock raising, and fishing. These activities produce the country's chief exports, mostly destined for markets on the West African coast.

At independence, Mali established an economy that eventually had parastatals responsible for virtually every aspect of the country's economic life. A national currency, the Mali franc, was issued in 1962, but by 1967 French aid was solicited for propping it up. During the Keita years, the first five-year development plan was launched; its aim was developing the rural economy and light industries. This plan achieved 67 percent of its objectives, and under it a number of important agricultural schemes were launched including Opération Riz, Opération Coton, Opération Arachide, and others. These rural development operations were expanded during the subsequent two five-year development plans. They now include in addition to those already mentioned, Opération Haute Vallée, Mali Sud, and Opération Mil.

During the 1960s, Mali made considerable progress in agricultural production. However, the droughts in the early 1970s and the mid-1980s, and erratic rainfall in other years, greatly reduced production. Several other important factors have served to keep agricultural productivity

Peul cattle being herded across the Diaka River (photo by author)

TABLE 6.1   Gross Domestic Product by Economic Activity, 1981 and 1982

	1981	1982
Agriculture, hunting, forestry, and fishing	349.4	388.8
Mining and quarrying	48.2	53.8
Manufacturing		
Electricity, gas and water	3.8	4.7
Construction	41.5	42.0
Trade, restaurants, and hotels	106.7	120.9
Transport, storage, and communications	21.0	25.2
Finance, insurance, real estate, and business services	9.8	12.5
Government services	52.5	58.1
Other community, social, and personal services	18.3	23.0
Sub-total	651.2	728.9
Statistical discrepancy	8.7	4.0
GDP in purchaser's values	659.9	732.9

Note: Figures in billions of Malian francs (MF); 700 MF = U.S. $1 (1983).

Sources: Mali, Africa South of the Sahara 1988, London, Europa Publications, Ltd., 1987, and Mali, National Accounts Statistics, New York, United Nations, 1987.

down. These include artificially low and fixed producer prices and a gradual abandonment of farming by the young.[4]

The average annual increase in Mali's gross domestic product (GDP) was on the order of 4.1 percent between 1973 and 1983, representing an improvement over the 3.1 percent annual increase that prevailed between 1965 and 1973. The average annual income is $200, a figure that is somewhat misleading because incomes in Bamako, the capital, are considerably higher. Mali's gross national product for most of the 1980s was $1.0 billion annually, translating into $140 per head. This makes Mali one of the poorest countries in the world (see Table 6.1). During the 1980s, some 83 percent of the labor force was engaged in farming and fishing, generally at a subsistence level. This compared with 93 percent in the mid-1960s. Only 140,000 Malians are salaried, half of them in the government bureaucracy or parastatals. This is an extremely low figure for wage employment. It is estimated that some 1 million Malians live outside of the country, with some 40,000 in France. The majority of the remainder are in neighboring coastal countries, especially the Ivory Coast. The remittances that Malians send home amount to some $23 million annually, which offsets one-third of the trade deficit. Pensions paid to some 13,000 veterans (anciens combattants) who served in the French armed forces also constitute an important source of external hard currency income. During the 1980s, the government, under pressure from donors, the World Bank, the International Monetary Fund, and the West African Monetary Union, which Mali rejoined in 1984, moved to liberalize the economy and abolish some of the parastatals. By 1989, Mali had abolished a number of the least profitable parastatals and was moving to eliminate additional ones. Meanwhile, despite incentives in the form of grants and loans from external donors, private enterprise was not taking hold to the degree hoped for.[5]

AGRICULTURE

Mali's staple food crops are millet, sorghum, maize, and rice. Fish and livestock products prominently figure in the national economy, as do the production of cash crops such as cotton, peanuts, tobacco, and sugar. Agricultural production has been hard hit by successive droughts, the rural to urban migration of the young, and institutional failings such as the payment of artificially low producer prices to farmers for food crops through the state marketing board, the Office des Produits Agricoles du Mali (OPAM). Fixed producer prices had first been instituted under the Keita government as means of maximizing profit for the state for cash crops and of providing food staples to politically important urban populations at artificially low prices. There were predictable consequences to the policy. Underpaid for their labors, farmers curtailed production to subsistence levels for food crops or else sold their surplus on the parallel market operated by a number of enterprising merchants. In 1975, for example, OPAM paid farmers 32 Malian francs (MF) for a kilo of millet. The going price in Senegal was the equivalent of 70 MF. Producers of rice in Mali were paid 40 MF per kilo whereas those in the Ivory Coast received the equivalent of 130–150 MF. The ability to market crops on the black market at considerably higher prices led to an outflow of food crops to neighboring countries. Private merchants involved in this trade were also able to provide farmers with credit to purchase equipment and loans against future crops with which to buy a range of consumer goods, advantages not offered by OPAM.

In 1983, the government began to reduce OPAM's role in agricultural marketing. However, this did not lead to the expected increase in productivity. Poor rainfall was one reason, but an equally important reason was the abandonment of farming by many who see it as an unprofitable enterprise. Those who remain on the farm continue to sell their surplus on the parallel market if they can or else produce only enough to feed themselves and their families. In the latter instance, they obtain the money necessary to pay annual head taxes and purchase necessities such as sugar, spices, and clothing with remittances sent by their children who are working either in Bamako or abroad.

A number of development programs in Mali have stressed cash crops, principally cotton and peanuts. During the 1960s and 1970s, those farmers who converted to these crops fared better financially than their neighbors who produced millet, sorghum, and maize. However, by the 1980s these differentials in income were leveled because of lowered international prices and shortages in rainfall that adversely affected production. Peanut production has steadily fallen in Mali because of conversion to better paying crops such as cotton and millet. The conversion of acreage to cash crops, which was strongly fostered by the government, also led to shortfalls in cereal production during the 1970s and 1980s.

The Office du Niger, which has regularly run deficits, presently has 131,000 acres of land under irrigation. In 1986, a major plan was implemented in that office to overhaul its management and to increase the total number of acres under cultivation to 247,000. This effort was heavily financed by France and the Federal Republic of Germany.

Mali is one of the major livestock producers in West Africa. Before the drought of the 1970s, there were 6 million cattle and 14 million goats and sheep, figures that were subsequently reduced by 30 percent by the drought. By the late 1970s, these figures had recovered to 5.8 million and 11.5 million respectively, following a government-sponsored program to rebuild the national herds. This included a temporary suspension of livestock exports that went into effect in 1975. However, some of these gains were nullified by the drought of the 1980s, which also witnessed a movement southward of livestock production from the north, which had become increasingly arid. By 1989, a few years of good rains had helped to return the national herd to normal levels.

Prior to the construction of the Markala Bridge and Dam, fish migrated up the Niger to Bamako and beyond. The dam effectively prevented these annual migrations and limited meaningful fishing to the lower stretches of the river. Mopti rapidly became the center of the fishing industry in Mali and during the 1960s and 1970s benefited from a number of development programs, some sponsored by the Food and Agriculture Organization (FAO) of the United Nations. The Bozo and Somono fishermen were organized into cooperatives and provided with motorized canoes. Losses through spoilage and insects used to be quite high, but an FAO-sponsored project greatly improved handling procedures and led to a marked reduction in such losses. In addition, a fish-processing and -canning factory was built in Mopti and the Mopti port was greatly improved.[6] The annual catch in nondrought years is of the order of 5,000 metric tons, a significant portion of which is exported

Bozo fishermen on the Diaka River near Lake Debo (photo by author)

Dried fish being brought into the port of Mopti (photo by author)

as dried fish to the Ivory Coast. In drought years, the catch has fallen by about 10 percent.

Aware of the failings of agricultural policies during the 1960s and 1970s, the government sought in the 1980s to remedy producer-price problems, develop extension services, and reduce the state's role in marketing. During the 1980s, Mali's annual productivity figures for various food and cash crops were heavily influenced by good harvests

A portion of Bamako's central market (photo by author)

in the areas of the Opérations de Développement Rural, autonomous administrative organizations, begun in 1974, whose purpose is to encourage and facilitate the production of one or more crops in a defined geographic area of the country. Some, such as the Mali Sud operation in the southern part of the country, are integrated projects that are focused on both cotton and cereal production. Both the Mali Sud and the Opération Haute Vallée have been responsible for the increase in Mali's cotton production in recent years.

Despite the development operations and the reforms in agricultural marketing, cereal shortfalls have been the rule throughout the 1980s. In 1983 and 1984, Mali had a shortfall of 150,000 tons in cereal, a figure that climbed to 480,000 tons in 1985, following the drought. These shortfalls have been covered for the most part by aid from outside donors, including the United States, which has regularly met much of Mali's cereal deficit with grain shipments given under the auspices of Public Law 480. On average, Mali produced 900,000 tons of millet, 120,000 tons of rice, 90,000 tons of maize, and 100,000 tons of peanuts per year during the 1980s. Cotton production was around 50,000 tons on average and sugarcane 107,000 tons. Significant proportions of the cash crops were used during the 1960s and early 1970s to pay off loans and grants from the Soviet Union and other Eastern bloc countries.

INDUSTRY

Industry occupies a relatively small place in Mali's economy, accounting for only 18 percent of the GDP. Most industries have been established around local raw materials. Parastatals account for most industrial development; in 1981, they were responsible for 90 percent of industrial output. Throughout the 1980s, the government attempted to reduce the role of the state in industry but had only moderate success. In 1982, there were close to forty parastatals, employing 15,000 people and registering annual losses of 9.8 billion Malian francs. The most successful state-owned industries have been those that meet high levels of domestic need. These include the cement factory at Diamou in the Kayes region, constructed with the assistance of the Soviet Union, the match and cigarette factories in Bamako, constructed with the help of the People's Republic of China, and the textile factory at Ségou, also constructed by the Chinese. Less successful have been a canning factory at Baguineda, constructed by Yugoslavia, and a ceramics factory in Bamako, built by North Korea. Cotton gins, rice-processing plants, and a sugar refinery at Dougabougou in the Office du Niger have been profitably run. Mali also has an abattoir in Bamako that functions effectively and one in Gao that is not used.

During the 1980s, a number of private entrepreneurs moved into areas of light industry, such as furniture making and printing. However, Mali has yet to attract the necessary capital to encourage the development of larger privately owned industries. The failure of many of the parastatals is a partial reason, as is the risk involved in investing in the country. Many of the parastatals failed because of limited markets for their products, inability to compete in terms of price and quality with similar products produced outside of the country, undercapitalization, overstaffing, and corruption. Private external investors as well as Malian investors are aware that even if the last three determinants of failure are removed, there is but a limited market. The size of Mali's internal market for certain manufactures is often too small to support industries that solely depend on it.[7]

During his first official visit to the United States in early October 1988, President Traoré made a strong bid for U.S. firms to invest in existing Malian industries and to set up new ones.[8] The new fiscal code in Mali permits the expatriation of all profits for the first several years and provides a number of inducements and tax abatements. However, Mali's long history of a socialist state-run economy and the continued existence of the principal structures of that economy, coupled with all of the problems and risks associated with investing in industries in the country, are major deterrents to venture capitalists. Although President

Traoré received considerable praise from the Reagan administration for his courageous private-sector initiatives, and *L'Essor* back in Bamako headlined the president's visit as "Opération Séduction,"[9] no major U.S. investors have thus far come forward to invest. In fact, the only major industrial investment in Mali by a U.S. firm in the late 1980s was made by a Utah-based mining concern, which contracted with the Malian government to mine gold fields in the western part of the country.

Mali's principal industrial achievements of the 1980s remain the two hydroelectric dams, Sélingué, which was constructed on the San-karani River in the southwestern part of the country, and Manantali, which was built on the Bafing River to the west. Sélingué has the capacity to produce 44.8 megawatts of electricity and has largely solved what had become a chronic shortage of electricity in Bamako. The Manantali Dam, part of which became operational in 1988, has not only the capacity to meet all of Mali's electricity needs for the foreseeable future but also enough to allow Mali to export electricity as well. It was constructed as part of the development plan for the Senegal River Valley of the Organisation pour la Mise-en-Valeur du Fleuve Sénégal (OMVS). However, although the dam was capable of holding back water, the hydroelectric turbines had not yet been installed in late 1988. A companion, the Diama Dam on the lower Senegal River, was constructed to prevent salt water from moving upriver. Great hopes have been placed on these dams by Mali, Senegal, and Mauritania, with Mali seeing in the dams an opportunity for an outlet to the sea and irrigation that will lead to greatly increased agricultural productivity. Funding for both of these dams has come from a wide group of donors, including France, West Germany, the European Development Fund, and oil-producing Arab countries, which all together have contributed 40 percent of the $700 million required. Development experts are still divided over whether the two dams will in fact lead to the expected increased agricultural productivity through irrigation. Many are of the opinion that flood-recession agriculture, now practiced along the river, will have to be gradually phased out through a lengthy transition period before irrigated agriculture replaces it. For this reason, Manantali has the capacity to simulate floods and formal plans between the three countries call for a continuance of artificial flooding for ten years to permit flood-recession agriculture.[10] Some 11,000 Malian peasants were displaced by the construction of the Manantali Dam. USAID provided the funds for their relocation.

MINING

Mali does not possess great mineral wealth, except for gold deposits, which are found in the *cercles* of Kenieba, Kangaba, and Yanfolila. Gold mining in these areas has been carried out since ancient times and still is by local populations, using shallow pits, during the dry season. During the 1960s, the government unsuccessfully attempted to set up gold-mining cooperatives among the peasants. Since then, the Soviet Union has provided Mali with technical advice in exploring the regions of ancient gold deposits, particularly in Kenieba and Yanfolila. However, in 1987 the Mali government and a French mining company, Bureau de Recherche Géologique et Minière, set up a joint gold-mining venture in Loulo, in the Kayes region, and in 1988 the Canadian gold-mining company, Sikamann Gold Resources, obtained a 196–square mile gold mining concession in Mali.[11] During the 1980s, some 500 kilograms of gold were produced annually. Most of the gold mined by local peasants does not figure in official statistics and is smuggled out of the country, often with pilgrims going to Mecca. There, it is exchanged for Western manufactures, especially wristwatches and transistor radios.

Mali has deposits of bauxite, copper, iron, nickel, manganese, and phosphates, all of varying quality, which have not yet been exploited because of the lack of infrastructure and the country's landlocked geographic position. Marble is presently mined at Bafoulabé and limestone quarried at Diamou, where the Soviets constructed a cement factory in 1969. The Tilemsi phosphate mine in Gao produces 2,000 tons annually, and it is hoped to eventually raise this level to 125,000 tons per year for use in a fertilizer plant. The salt mines at Taoudeni produce some 4,000 tons of rock salt annually.

TRANSPORTATION

At independence, Mali was heavily dependent on the 804-mile-long Koulikoro-Dakar railway for access to the sea and had only a small infrastructure of all-weather and paved roads. The rupture of the Mali Federation led to the closure of the border between Mali and Senegal and left Mali with an internal railway system that effectively had no repair yards; they were at Thies in Senegal. Mali quickly built repair yards at Korofina in Bamako and placed the railway under a state-owned company, the Régie des Chemins de Fer du Mali. At the same time, Mali quickly developed a paved road system south to the Ivory Coast in order to assure itself of an alternative outlet to the sea. The 403 miles of railway in Mali have regularly been upgraded and new equipment added, the latest being 100 goods wagons that were donated by Canada in 1986.[12] Passengers and goods are carried to and from Bamako and the western part of the country, but there is less dependence on the line for importing and exporting goods through the port of Dakar than there was prior to 1960.

One of the most impressive development achievements during Mali's first thirty years of independence has been the construction of paved roads. In 1960, there were few paved stretches in the country; the principal ones were between Bamako and Ségou (147 miles), San and Mopti (126 miles), and Bamako and Bougouni (102 miles). During the 1960s, the 125-mile-long road between Ségou and San was paved and a bridge built over the Bani River, replacing the ferry. The 185 miles between Bougouni and the border of the Ivory Coast were also paved, as were the stretches between San and Koutiala and the latter and the Upper Volta (Burkina Faso) border. The European Development Fund financed many of these road-building projects. Road building continued in the 1970s with the paving of the 81 miles between Koutiala and Sikasso in the south and the reconstruction of the old paved road between Bamako and Ségou. A major road-building achievement of the 1980s has been the construction of a paved road between Mopti-Sevare and Gao, a distance of 359 miles. This road brings the eastern part of the country into easy contact with the rest of Mali for the first time. Prior to its construction, there existed a poor track that required from two to three days to traverse. The construction of this new road was financed by the Organization of Petroleum Exporting Countries (OPEC) Fund for International Development and the Arab Bank for Economic Development in Africa. In addition to these major paved roads, shorter ones have been constructed in the central part of the country in conjunction with a number of development projects. A paved road from Kayes to Bamako is planned in the future as part of a Dakar-Lagos road link.

By the 1980s, many of Mali's major paved roads that had been constructed during the 1960s and 1970s had fallen into serious disrepair through a lack of regular maintenance. In 1985, the International Development Association approved $48.6 million toward the $73.4 million required to rehabilitate some of the main paved-road networks and to rebuild parts of the paved road between Bamako and the Ivory Coast border. The latter road is extremely important economically because it carries roughly 58 percent of Mali's imports and 65 percent of its exports.

Air Mali, established at independence, long served the internal air-transport needs of the country and in addition had regularly scheduled flights to Europe and other parts of Africa. Air Mali operated with a chronically large deficit, and in March 1986 it was partially liquidated. It carried some 75,000 passengers annually during the 1980s and 600,000 metric tons of freight. The Air Mali fleet during the 1980s consisted of one Ilyushian-18, DC-3s, Antinov-24s, a Boeing 727, and a Boeing 737. There were two serious air disasters involving Air Mali planes, one in August 1974, when an Ilyushian-18 crashed near Ouagadougou in Upper

Volta on a flight from Jidda, Saudi Arabia, and a second in February 1985, when an Antinov-24 crashed after takeoff from Timbuctoo.[13] Internal air transport in Mali since the down scaling of Air Mali has been provided by small private carriers, using four- and six-seater planes. A number of foreign carriers connect Bamako with Europe and other parts of Africa. The opening of the new paved road to Gao has greatly reduced dependence on internal air flights to the eastern part of the country. In 1973, a new airport was opened outside of Bamako at Sénou, and its terminal was completed in December 1975.

Transport on the Niger River has diminished in importance with the development of air links and road networks in the interior. In the 1960s, the Federal Republic of Germany gave Mali a new riverboat, the *General Soumaré*, and in the 1970s a newer boat, the *Kanga Moussa* was added. Both carry passengers and freight between Koulikoro and Gao when the river is navigable, from August through January.

DEVELOPMENT AND FINANCE

Mali has had three five-year development programs. The first plan, 1961–1966, was aimed at the development of infrastructure and modernizing and developing the rural economy and transitional industries. In addition, the plan focused on mining research, transportation, and a broad range of educational, health, and cultural objectives. Under this plan, several important agricultural schemes were begun, including Opération Riz, Opération Coton, Opération Arachide, and others. This plan put into place many of the structures of Mali's socialist state-run economy. Mali's second five-year plan, 1974–1979, was aimed at revamping the banking and financial systems. The French, who had assumed a major responsibility for the banking system and the issuance of the Malian franc after the 1967 Franco-Malian financial accords, were given an increased role in the central bank.

The 1981–1985 five-year plan was intended to stimulate production and improve the efficiency of economic management. Its goal was to maintain an annual growth of the GDP at 5 percent, a goal that was not reached. The plan called for the establishment of a fund to develop underground-water resources and to exploit fossil fuels, hydroelectric power, and other forms of renewable energy. The most important achievement of the plan was the completion of the Sélingué Dam. The total amount projected for this plan was 930 billion Mali francs.

In 1962, Mali left the franc zone and issued its own currency. During the first few years that this franc was in circulation, Mali printed money to cover budgetary gaps. In 1967, Mali signed monetary accords with France and devalued the Malian franc by 50 percent. A further devaluation of 12.5 percent took place in 1969. Mali returned to the West African Monetary Union in 1984 and thereafter the Communauté Financière Africaine (CFA) franc became the national currency.

Between 1970 and 1973, Mali launched a Programme Triennial, whose aim was fiscal and economic reform. Although the program did not achieve all of its objectives, it did limit spending levels. Since the late 1960s, Mali has drawn heavily on French subsidies to cover chronic operating deficits. By 1983, the annual deficit stood at 13.77 billion CFA francs ($35 million) and has steadily climbed ever since. The 1987 budget was 78.6 billion CFA francs and covered only operating expenses (see Table 6.2). Mali is almost entirely dependent on external sources for capital expenditures. During the 1980s, foreign assistance in the form of loans, grants, and subsidies amounted to slightly more than the annual operating budget of the government. Mali has been the recipient of a great deal of assistance from a variety of bilateral and international donors during the thirty years of its independence. This assistance has consisted not only of money and material but also of technical personnel, who have been engaged in a broad spectrum of development programs. Mali's principal sources of aid have been France, the European Economic Community, the USSR, and the PRC.

During the late 1980s, the International Monetary Fund (IMF) and the World Bank played an increasingly important role in the restructuring of Mali's economy. In 1986, France provided a credit line of 7 billion CFA francs ($20 million) to support the IMF adjustment program agreed to by Mali. A key ingredient of Mali's economic reform program is the intentional delay in payment of salaries to civil servants and employees of parastatals. Although this has eased Mali's monthly cash flow problems, it has also been extremely unpopular with government workers.

In August 1988, the IMF gave Mali a $45 million line of credit in order to help the economic restructuring process. By early 1989, Mali had made moves to dismantle the Société Malienne d'Importation et d'Exportation (SOMIEX), the state monopoly importer and exporter, and to strip Air Mali of its monopoly protections. The prices of many items, including cereals, were liberalized by March 1989. However, during a visit to Mali in March 1989, representatives of the IMF and the World Bank expressed unhappiness about the slow pace of the restructuring effort. The Malians claimed that this lack of progress was due to a dearth of foreign investment, government fears about the consequences for consumers of dismantling SOMIEX, and the loss of revenues due to a drop in the world price of cotton. The Malian government also cited corruption and a need to market the country's products better as major impediments to the restructuring of its economy; the government called on friendly countries and international institutions to assist it in these

TABLE 6.2   National Budgets, 1981 to 1983

	1981	1982	1983
REVENUE[a]			
Subtotal	**87,281**	**107,060**	**112,992**
Adjustment to cash basis	280	−1,725	−3,820
Total current revenue	**87,561**	**105,335**	**109,172**
Capital revenue	55	24	38
Total revenue	**87,616**	**105,359**	**109,210**
EXPENDITURES[b]			
General public services	23,395	25,174	26,948
Defense	17,217	19,302	20,486
Education	22,646	23,970	26,087
Health	8,020	6,332	6,598
Social security and welfare	3,674	11,371	11,868
Housing and community amenities	—	142	128
Other community and social services	1,839	2,120	2,068
Economic services	8,015	18,616	18,284
General administration, regulation, and research	1,013	1,109	997
Agriculture, forestry, and fishing	7,002	12,338	10,893
Mining, manufacturing, and construction	—	189	252
Transport and communications	—	4,980	6,142
Other purposes	4,110	6,926	7,786
Unclassified expenditure in government accounts	22,898	2,734	1,740
Subtotal	**111,814**	**117,227**	**121,993**
Adjustment to cash basis	−15,937	8,945	13,676
Total expenditure	**95,877**	**126,172**	**135,666**

Notes: Figures in millions of Malian francs. 700 MF = U.S. $1.

Figures refer to the consolidated accounts of the central government and certain government agencies. Figures for 1981 exclude the operations of the National Social Security Institute.

The budgets for 1984–1987 were as follows: 1984: Revenue—47,200, Expenditure—52,900; 1985: Revenue—61,800, Expenditure—64,200; 1986: Revenue—69,180, Expenditure—69,080; 1987: Budget balanced at 78,600. (All figures in millions of francs CFA: 350 CFA = U.S. $1.)

[a]Excluding grants received (million Mali francs): 56,526 in 1981; 61,160 in 1982; 81,023 in 1983.

[b]Excluding net lending (million Mali francs): −246 in 1981; 44 in 1982; 248 in 1983. Figures also exclude unclassified expenditure of foreign grants and loans outside government accounts (million Mali francs): 77,800 in 1981; 103,400 in 1982; 123,400 in 1983.

Source: Mali, *Africa South of the Sahara 1988,* London, Europa Publications, Ltd., 1987, and *Government Finance Statistics Yearbook,* International Monetary Fund, 1987.

areas. Outside observers noted that there were significant political consequences in dismantling large parastatals, given the large numbers of people employed in them.

U.S. AID TO MALI

U.S. economic assistance to Mali, which began in 1961, amounted to $350 million by 1988.[14] Of this amount, some $90 million was for food aid during the drought periods of 1970–1974 and 1984–1985. During fiscal year 1988, the United States provided Mali with $35 million. Of this amount, $9.1 million was for food aid, $19.6 million for specific projects, $1.8 million for assistance in combatting locusts, and $5 million in support for economic policy reform projects.

The U.S. aid program for Mali in the late 1980s emphasized three principal themes: policy reform (especially liberalization of agricultural prices and markets, increased incentives for the private sector, and support for budget restructuring); food security (through research in higher yielding, drought-resistant crops, better agricultural technology, and support for child survival and family planning); and management improvement, especially through extensive training programs. Between 1985 and 1988, the United States provided Mali with $24.5 million to support economic reform, including the voluntary reduction of excessive government employment, support for privatization, and reform of tax and trade policies to encourage economic growth.[15]

U.S. assistance to the Malian armed forces dates to the early 1960s, when several of today's senior officers received training in the United States, but was suspended by Mali during the late 1960s, as President Modibo Keita's radical policies took hold. It was resumed in 1979 and currently consists of a training program for eight to ten Malian military officers per year. An English-language laboratory was established for these trainees in 1988 in Bamako. The program is funded at $150,000 annually.

FOREIGN TRADE

During the 1980s, Mali's principal imports in terms of value were petroleum products, industrial products, miscellaneous manufactures, and machinery. Cereals, sugar, and cotton yarn and fabrics together accounted for 10 percent of the value of imports. Mali's principal export is cotton, followed by live animals, fats and oils, the latter being peanut oil. In terms of exports, the Ivory Coast is the country's chief trading partner, followed by France and the Federal Republic of Germany. The value of exports to the Federal Republic of Germany has in certain years

TABLE 6.3   Mali's External Trade According to Principal Trading Partners, 1980 and 1981

	1980	1981
IMPORTS		
France	12,685	21,703
Ivory Coast	15,193	16,403
Senegal	4,302	10,703
Federal Republic of Germany	4,622	10,044
Ecuador	—	2,784
U.S.A.	1,440	1,817
Other	13,676	9,730
Total[a]	51,918	73,184
EXPORTS		
Ivory Coast	4,782	8,713
Federal Republic of Germany	3,117	4,954
France	6,001	4,206
China	2,931	2,064
Japan	1,416	2,057
United Kingdom	2,231	1,926
Other	4,336	4,532
Total[a]	24,814	28,452

Note: Figures in millions of CFA francs; 350 CFA francs = U.S. $1 (1983).

[a]Total includes several other countries not listed, with which the value of trade was small.

Source: Mali, *Africa South of the Sahara 1988*, London, Europa Publications, Ltd., 1988, and Banque Centrale des Etats de L'Afrique de l'Ouest, Abidjan, Ivory Coast.

slightly exceeded that of exports to France. In terms of imports, France accounts for a third of the value of what Mali receives, followed by the Ivory Coast, the Federal Republic of Germany, and Nigeria (see Table 6.3).

Mali has consistently run a trade deficit, whose causes are multiple. During the 1960s, total exports were in the range of 4 billion CFA francs annually while imports ran around 12 billion CFA francs. Although exports tripled between 1969 and 1974 because of higher prices for cotton, the need to import cereals because of the drought and the rise in petroleum prices elevated import values to almost three times that of exports. The trade deficit eased somewhat during the 1970s and by 1977 was equal to one-quarter of export receipts. The trade deficit continued to worsen during the 1980s because of the fall in the world price of cotton, the impact of the drought of the mid-1980s, and the second round of rises in petroleum products (see Table 6.4). The cumulative trade deficit in the mid-1980s stood at 67.6 billion CFA francs (see Table 6.5). Two-thirds of this trade deficit are offset by the remittances

TABLE 6.4   Mali's External Trade According to Commodities, 1980 and 1981

	1980	1981
IMPORTS		
Cereals	2,135	2,441
Sugar	3,451	3,406
Refined petroleum products	17,944	22,124
Electrical machinery	1,478	2,639
Nonelectrical machinery	5,174	5,214
Road transport equipment	4,807	5,473
Other industrial products	11,777	29,074
Chemicals	3,240	6,598
Miscellaneous manufactured articles	8,537	22,476
Cotton yarn and fabrics	495	4,946
Total[a]	51,918	76,975
EXPORTS		
Live animals	4,671	6,575
Oil-cakes	300	501
Shea butter	597	193
Hides and skins	280	447
Cotton (ginned)	16,640	17,470
Fats and oils	741	2,135
Total[a]	24,814	28,452

Note: Figures in million CFA francs; 350 CFA = U.S. $1 (1983).

[a]Totals include other commodities whose traded volume is not substantial.

Source: Mali, Africa South of the Sahara 1988, London, Europa Publications, Ltd., 1988, and Banque Centrale des Etats de l'Afrique de l'Ouest, Abidjan, Ivory Coast.

TABLE 6.5   Total Value of Imports and Exports, by Year

	Imports	Exports	
1980	51,918	24,814	(cotton 16,640)
1981	76,975	28,452	(cotton 17,470)
1982	109,200	47,900	(cotton 17,050)
1983	134,600	62,900	(cotton 25,950)
1984	160,900	89,400	(cotton 39,400)
1985	187,700	81,100	(cotton 32,800)
1986	151,700	66,400	(cotton 24,000)

Note: Figures in millions of CFA francs; 350 CFA = U.S. $1 (1983).

Source: International Financial Statistics, International Monetary Fund, and Mali, Africa South of the Sahara 1988, London, Europa Publications, Ltd., 1988.

of emigrants and by foreign aid. During the mid-1980s, the latter amounted to some $281.3 million per year from non-Communist countries alone. This figure does not include French budgetary supports and payments supports, which are almost equal to the annual government budget.

The country has benefited from the cancellation of bilateral debts, particularly during the drought of the mid-1980s. In 1985, Mali's external debt was $960 million, equivalent to 96 percent of the GNP. This figure compares with an external debt of $422 million in 1977. Mali requested a rescheduling of its foreign debt in 1987 and agreed to a broad program of structural changes requested by the International Monetary Fund.[16] Despite this, there is little prospect that the country will be able to get along without outside financial aid for the foreseeable future.

ATTEMPTS TO PRIVATIZE

The ongoing collapse of Mali's state-run economy, the unwillingness of external donors, particularly France, to continue propping it up, and the requirements of the IMF and World Bank for continued assistance forced President Traoré to make a break with Mali's well-entrenched socialist tradition, at least in the economic sphere. Many Malians see Traoré's drive to privatize as the latest stratagem in his politics of pragmatism. As they view it, the public sector is incapable of absorbing any more personnel and in fact needs to be reduced. The creation of a private sector gives the government a solution by enabling it to tell people to find jobs in this private sector, which by the late 1980s was still in its infancy.

Since the mid-1980s, Traoré has moved forward with a program of dismantling unprofitable state enterprises (for example, Air Mali), opening the country to Western investors, and encouraging private enterprise. During Traoré's October 1988 visit to the United States, his press attaché, Tiona Mathieu Koné, said that Mali had reached "a decisive turning point" and had formulated a national strategy to develop the private sector and encourage Western investments. He added that "we have learned a bitter lesson from our heavy centralized state-run economy," and he characterized SOMIEX, the import-export parastatal, as a failure because of "inefficient, poor management."[17]

The United States, France, the IMF, the World Bank, and other Western donors have encouraged Mali in its attempts to privatize major areas of the economy and have provided financial supports to buttress the government from the unavoidable and politically dangerous consequences. Introducing capitalist concepts into a country that for the first quarter century of its existence strongly embraced socialism is no easy matter. The late President Modibo Keita's socialist options were not discarded when he was overthrown in 1968 but were continued without fanfare by the military government well into the early 1980s. This has had a major influence on how Malians perceive economic problems and their solutions. Changing these perceptions will take time, as will getting young people accustomed to the idea that completion of higher education no longer confers on them an entitlement of government employment.

7

Mali's International Relations

Although Mali is a poor country with a relatively small population, it has maintained an active and influential position in international affairs. In part, this has been a compensatory mechanism for protecting specific interests and for ensuring continued sovereignty. Mali is a member of a large number of political and economic groupings and its diplomats and administrators have served in leadership positions in a number of them, including the United Nations (UN), the Organization of African Unity (OAU), the Comité Permanent Inter-Etats de Lutte Contre la Secheresse dans le Sahel (CILSS), and the Communauté Economique de l'Afrique de l'Ouest (CEAO).

Since independence, Mali has been a member of the group of nonaligned nations, identified with progressive African governments and movements, maintained a special relationship with France because of financial necessity and historical circumstances, and cultivated close relations with countries of the Communist bloc. Mali has not pursued a pro-Western foreign policy but rather has sought neutral ground or else has come down on the side of the Communist bloc. The latter is exhibited by its support of Cuban intervention in Angola, the Soviet invasion of Afghanistan, its diplomatic recognition of North Korea but not South Korea, and the close economic and cultural ties it has maintained with a number of Eastern bloc countries. It trod a neutral position with regard to the Sino-Soviet split and clearly profited by doing so, receiving material aid from both sides.

Mali has been an active voice in African, Islamic, and Third World politics. In these arenas, it has generally avoided choosing sides and has stayed on good terms with competing camps and groups. Although the country is officially laic, its large Moslem population necessitates involvement in Islamic issues. It has maintained cordial relations with the Palestine Liberation Organization (PLO) and Libya while at the same time staying on good terms with moderate Arab states, such as Saudi Arabia and Egypt. Mali also maintained diplomatic relations with Israel until 1973 and was the beneficiary of a number of Israeli foreign-assistance programs. Relations were broken at that time in solidarity with the Arab member states of the OAU following the Yom Kippur War.

RELATIONS WITH FRANCE

At independence in 1960, Mali attempted to make a clear break with its old colonial master, a strategy that ultimately failed. In dramatic contrast to some of its neighbors, such as Senegal, Upper Volta, Niger, and the Ivory Coast, Mali quickly Africanized all government services, so that only a small handful of French advisers remained in place. Now, three decades after independence, Mali is more than ever before dependent on France for bilateral aid and annual budgetary supports, without which the government would collapse.

The rupture of the Mali Federation in 1960, and Modibo Keita's perception of France's having played a major role in that breakup, placed a shadow over Franco-Malian relations. In addition, Mali strongly opposed France's Algerian policy at the time and viewed the continued stationing of some 2,200 French troops in Mali as furthering the cause of this policy and compromising Mali's sovereignty. After much negotiation, these troops were finally grouped at Kati near Bamako during 1960 and 1961 and withdrawn by September 1961. Although France offered to sponsor Mali for admission to the UN, this was thwarted by Mali's vitriolic denunciation of France's Algerian policy; consequently, Mali was sponsored by Tunisia and Ceylon, becoming the ninety-eighth member of the organization.[1]

Despite this difficult start, Keita entered into negotiations with the French in 1962 that eventually led to the ratifying of a number of cultural, economic, and financial accords. However, while negotiations over these accords were going on, Mali announced its intentions of withdrawing from the franc zone and issuing its own currency. In addition, at the trial of Fily Dabo Sissoko and his associates in 1962, accused of inciting the riot over the issuance of the new currency, it was alleged that they had been in complicity with the French embassy. The French were also accused of helping the Tuareg rebels in the north of the country. Despite the less than congenial atmosphere that surrounded relations between the two countries at this time, Mali made a conscious effort to improve relations later on, in large part because of necessity.

In 1965, new Franco-Malian financial negotiations were begun, but they were stalled for varying periods until they were resumed in 1967.

By this time, Mali had hesitantly become increasingly dependent on France for its economic and financial survival. Without publicly acknowledging this ever-growing dependency, Keita launched domestic initiatives, such as the Cultural Revolution, to appease the radicals in the party. At the same time, his government was shrill in its condemnation of U.S. intervention in Vietnam and in its denunciation of neocolonialism and neoimperialism. In so doing, Keita attempted to place his Marxist-socialist purity in high profile while quietly taking life-saving financial help from the French.[2]

The Comité Militaire de Liberation Nationale (CMLN) and the civilian government of Moussa Traoré that have ruled Mali since the coup d'état of November 19, 1968, did not essentially alter Mali's foreign policy alignments. With respect to the former metropole, relations rapidly improved. Yoro Diakité, the vice president of the CMLN, paid an official visit to General de Gaulle in March 1969 to explain events in Mali, and, in January 1970, Yvon Bourges, the French secretary of state for foreign affairs, visited Bamako. President Moussa Traoré made a state visit to France in April 1972 and held talks with French President Georges Pompidou. These visits led to an intensification of high-level official contacts between Mali and France that culminated in the signing of financial and economic accords in 1973. Finally, President Valéry Giscard d'Estaing visited Mali February 11–13, 1977, marking the first time that a French president had come to the country since independence. This visit gave a new impetus for further cooperative efforts between the two countries. At the time, France was providing Mali with 30 percent of all bilateral aid and 20 percent of all foreign aid.

Throughout the 1980s, Mali and France have maintained extremely cordial relations, the Malians being particularly cautious not to disrupt them in any major way because of their extreme financial dependency on France. The French, for their part, enjoy certain trade preferences that help domestic industries in France. In January 1981, President Traoré paid an official visit to Paris for the purpose of requesting Mali's readmission to the West African Monetary Union and to discuss other issues of mutual importance. His requests were favorably received, and throughout the decade France continued to provide Mali with extensive support. In November 1986, French President François Mitterrand visited Mali for the purpose of reaching agreement on the provision of significant aid.

Only one small incident troubled the otherwise excellent relations between the two countries during the 1980s. This involved France's expulsion of 101 Malians in October 1986. The people expelled were those whose immigration papers were not in order or who were completing prison terms. The official Malian reaction to these expulsions was stronger than the French had anticipated, and no doubt injured national pride played a role. The French quickly moved to mollify the Malians, signing an agreement in January 1988 that provides for facilitating the rehabilitation of immigrant Malian workers. Under the terms of this agreement, the French provide immigrants who are to be repatriated with training and retraining courses and the Malian government makes available to them parcels of land for agricultural purposes. In addition, the French provide concessions in the fiscal and customs sectors for immigrants who are returned to Mali.[3]

Thirty years after independence, relations with France are excellent. The feelings of ordinary Malians toward the French have mellowed since independence, and in fact, some among the older generations now recall the colonial era with great nostalgia. The absence of large numbers of French nationals in the country and the fact that none of them occupy administrative or military positions has served to avoid local negative feelings toward them. This is in contrast to the situation in neighboring Senegal, where at independence there were 40,000 French nationals in the country, a number that by 1980 had only fallen to 18,000. At present, there are barely 400 French technical assistance personnel in Mali.

REGIONAL RELATIONS

Whereas a number of Mali's neighbors restricted their inter-African relationships during the 1960s to their own region and to other francophone African countries, Mali cast a wider net. Yet, even for Mali, the most important relationships remain regional in character. Mali shares borders with seven countries, and its dealings with some of them have at times been difficult. However, by the late 1980s, relations with all of these neighbors were excellent, even with Burkina Faso, with which Mali had gone to war on two occasions. With Burkina Faso, Mauritania, and Algeria, the improvements came about through the resolution of border disputes; with Senegal and the Ivory Coast, because they best serve mutual economic interests.

The breakup of the Mali Federation soured relations between Mali and Senegal and led to the closure of the border between them. The most significant impact of this was the blockade of the railway to the coast, a problem that Mali solved, as we have seen, by rapidly constructing a major road to the border with the Ivory Coast. Both countries soon realized that their best economic interests lay in cooperation, especially with regard to developing the Senegal River Basin. Two years after the rupture of relations, a Senegalese delegation visited Bamako with the aim of reestablishing diplomatic and commercial contacts. By 1963, the two countries had agreed on the reopening of the Dakar-Niger railway, and in June of that year they signed accords in Bamako normalizing their relations. Presidents Senghor and Keita met shortly thereafter at Kidira on the border to symbolize this normalization of relations. In demonstrating its commitment to this new era, Mali went as far as to expel Senegalese opposition groups that it had sheltered during the time when diplomatic relations with Senegal had been suspended.

During the ensuing years, the two countries were brought closer together out of a desire to develop the Senegal River Basin. Both realized that they had to demonstrate cooperation in order to attract outside donors and the tens of millions of dollars needed for the project. In 1968, they, along with Guinea and Mauritania, formed a regional organization known as the Organisation des Etats Riverains du Sénégal (OERS) for the purpose of promoting this project. In 1969, Guinea and Mali had disagreements, and in 1972 when Guinea quarreled with Senegal, Guinea withdrew from the organization. The three remaining countries then formed a successor organization known as the Organisation pour la Mise-en-Valeur du Fleuve Sénégal (OMVS). In 1988, Guinea expressed interest in rejoining the group.

The two major projects of the OMVS are the Manantali Dam in Mali and the Diama Dam in Senegal. Mali hopes that the former will provide it with an outlet to the sea (by making the Senegal River navigable most of the year) and huge amounts of hydroelectric power. Senegal sees in both dams an opportunity for massive irrigated agriculture, protection against drought, and a chance to become self-sufficient in food production.

Major economic interests of both Senegal and Mali are linked through the OMVS, and both countries have worked hard to maintain excellent bilateral relations. The presidents of each country have frequently visited the other's capital, beginning with the visit of President Senghor to Bamako in December 1965.

At the time of independence, the moderate government of the Ivory Coast, headed by Félix Houphouet-Boigny, was flanked by three radical states, Ghana, Guinea, and Mali. The Ivory Coast found it easiest to establish friendly relations with Mali, which came to depend on it for access to the sea with the closure of the Dakar-Niger railway. The Ivory Coast's booming economy has provided work to tens of thousands of Malians whose remittances help shore up Mali's own economy. Mali also desired friendly relations with the Ivory Coast because of those workers. This suited the interests of the Ivory Coast, which felt more secure having friendly relations with at least one of the three adjacent radical states. Over the years, both countries have maintained friendly relations; again, economics has played a major role in determining this. The Ivory Coast is a major trading partner of Mali, and during the

1980s purchased a third of Mali's exports annually. After France, the Ivory Coast was the chief source of Mali's imports, accounting for 20 percent of the value of imports annually. Thus, trade, access to the sea, and a mutual interest in migrant workers have played determining roles in forging the friendly relations between the two countries.

Mali's relations with Mauritania have been complex and not always friendly. At independence, relations between the two countries got off to a very bad start because of Malian designs on the eastern Hodh region of Mauritania, which was once part of the colony of the Sudan. In November 1960, the Malian government announced that over a four-month period serious incidents had taken place along the Mali-Mauritanian border, resulting in eleven deaths. It blamed Maures in Mauritania, who Mali charged were attempting to continue their exploitation of slaves in Mali. Morocco, which also had designs on Mauritanian territory, joined Mali in attempting to weaken and threaten Mauritania. During 1961 and 1962, President Keita made three official visits to Rabat, Morocco, to confer with King Hassan. In April 1962, the Mauritanians accused Mali and Morocco of planning to subvert their country by infiltrating forces from Malian soil. In an attempt to defuse the situation, the Mauritanians offered to send a goodwill mission to Bamako in May 1962, but President Keita refused to receive it. However, by August the Malians, realizing that their future economic interests lay with good relations with Mauritania, met the Mauritanians to discuss their common border problem.

In January 1963, both sides met in the southern Mauritanian town of Aioun-El-Atrous and agreed on the demarcation of the frontier. The actual border was then marked out on the ground at those points where there had been disagreement in the past. On February 16, 1963, President Keita met with President Moktar Ould Daddah of Mauritania in the Malian town of Kayes and concluded a treaty exactly defining the frontier between the two countries.[4] However, the frontier issue was not laid to rest by this treaty because over the years Maures from Mauritania have regularly descended into Mali and pillaged agricultural settlements for grain, particularly during periods of drought. Questions still remained about the frontiers agreed to in the 1963 treaty, and in June 1969, both sides met again in Bamako to discuss them. However, in August 1987, Abderhamane Maiga, Malian minister of territorial administration and development, held a working session with the Mauritanian minister of the interior, Djibril Ould Abdallahi, at which it was decided that the treaty frontiers would be maintained.[5]

Mauritania's role in the Senegal River Basin development scheme is crucial to Mali's best economic interests, and this has regularly overridden other bilateral concerns. These latter include the Malian designs on the Hodh region, a sense of solidarity with the black populations in southern Mauritania, which have been in regular conflict with the Arab-dominated government over their inferior status, and support for the Front Populaire pour la Libération de la Saguiat et Hamra et du Rio de Oro (POLISARIO Front), which is waging a protracted war in the western Sahara with Morocco for the independence of what was once the Spanish colony of Rio de Oro (Spanish Sahara). The Malians have recognized the POLISARIO but not the Sahrawi Arab Democratic Republic, as POLISARIO has named the territory. Mali condemned the joint Mauritanian-Moroccan invasion of the territory in 1976 and along with Nigeria facilitated Mauritania's withdrawal from the area at a meeting in Algiers in May 1979 at which POLISARIO and Mauritanian leaders were brought together.

Since independence, Mali has always sought to maintain friendly relations with Algeria, with which it shares a long border. The Tuareg rebellion of the early 1960s in northern Mali demonstrated how crucial Algeria's role was in maintaining Mali's control over its vast northern desert. Facilitating the relationship between the two countries is their similar socialist/progressive political orientation. The Malians and Algerians frequently met during the 1970s to discuss their 870-mile-long common border, and in May 1983 President Traoré traveled to Algiers to sign a treaty that settled the border issue in the spirit of the OAU charter, which recognized colonial boundaries as legitimate and as a guarantee of stability on the continent. During the same visit, Algeria agreed to send physicians to Mali and to admit Malians to Algerian technical schools. By April 1984, the actual demarcation of the border was completed in accordance with the 1983 agreement.

Both countries have regularly maintained high-level diplomatic contacts, as exemplified by the visit of the Algerian foreign minister to Bamako in late 1985. The two countries set up an Intergovernmental Committee that regularly meets to discuss issues of mutual concern. The sixth such committee meeting was held in Bamako in December 1986 to discuss agricultural and development projects in the areas near their common borders. The committee has also been concerned in recent years in the construction of a trans-Saharan highway, the Mopti-Gao portion of which was completed in 1986, the introduction of Algerian gas for domestic Malian consumption, and the fight against deforestation and the encroaching desert.[6]

Mali's relations with Niger have always been friendly and cordial, in large measure because there are no common border disputes nor major violations of the border by the nationals of either country. Tension between the two countries did arise at the time of the Sahelian drought during the early 1970s, when large numbers of Malian refugees fled to

Niger complaining that the Malian government was not doing anything to assist them. The arrival of these refugees placed a great strain on Nigerien resources, a situation that was rapidly alleviated by international aid. Malian indifference to these people aroused strong feelings among the Nigeriens, who have a sense of solidarity with the peoples of eastern Mali because many of them are from the same ethnic groups. The groups that live on both sides of the Mali-Niger border include not only the Tuareg but also the Djerma and Songhay.

The ethnic affinity of peoples in eastern Mali with those in Niger has always been a major political concern of the Malian government. It has attempted to deal with this issue by bringing representatives of these groups into key government and administrative positions and by maintaining a strong military presence in the region. In addition, the government has tried to maintain close communication and transportation links with the area and pushed hard to obtain funding for building a paved road between Mopti and Gao. This new artery now serves not only a practical purpose in transporting goods and people between Bamako and Gao but also a political one in bringing this outlying region closer to the political center of the country.

Mali's relations with Libya have been friendly but not close. Mali has maintained correct relations while exercising prudence in relating to Libya, whose ideology it does not share. Libya's involvement in the affairs of sub-Saharan African countries, particularly Chad, has made the Malians extremely cautious in dealing with Col. Muammar Qaddafi. Closer to home, Malians recall Libya's support in the late 1970s of a Senegalese dissident movement intent on overthrowing the government of President Senghor and replacing it with an Islamic republic. In 1980, Libya was implicated in recruiting Gambians for military training for the purpose of overthrowing the governments of Gambia and Senegal. Libya's growing involvement in neighboring Burkina Faso in the early 1980s gave the Malians serious cause for concern and probably contributed to Mali's military offensive against Burkina Faso in 1985.

There are several reasons why Mali needs to maintain cordial relations with Libya. Mali receives significant assistance from that country in the form of support for cultural and development programs. Several thousand Malian immigrant workers work in Libya and regularly send home remittances, which help the Malian economy. Finally, Mali is intimidated by the shadow of Tuareg dissidents who have been given military training in Libya and who are sheltered there. A deterioration of relations could lead Libya to mobilize this group, which could pose serious problems for the Malian government. Thus, severing diplomatic relations could be injurious to Mali on several counts. However, in January 1981, Mali expelled Libyan diplomats from Bamako without breaking diplomatic ties when the Libyan embassy was converted to a people's bureau. Relations deteriorated somewhat again in September 1985, when the Libyans expelled some 3,880 Malian workers. Colonel Qaddafi tried to repair the damage caused by these expulsions during a visit to Bamako in December 1985, while on a trip to several West African capitals.[7]

THE BORDER DISPUTE
WITH BURKINA FASO

Mali's most difficult relations have been with Burkina Faso (formerly, Upper Volta). These have focused on a border dispute in the region known as the Agacher or the Udalan, which measures some 100 miles long and twelve miles deep. In November 1974, both countries accused one another of border incursions in the disputed region. The border in this area was poorly defined during the colonial period because Upper Volta was established (1919), dismantled (1932), and finally reconstituted (1947), and in the process the disputed territory was given to the Sudan. Thus, the border became contestable. The two armies clashed over a period of several weeks in the region in 1974–1975, incurring few casualties. However, in November 1974 in the Voltaic town of Bob-Dioulasso, there was a serious riot against Malians in which it is estimated that several dozen men were killed. Although the OAU was unable to settle the dispute between the two countries, Togo, Senegal, Niger, and Guinea brought the two sides together for a cease-fire. However, the problem remained unresolved. Finally, on September 17, 1983, Thomas Sankara, a Voltaic military officer who had gained fame for his field role in the 1974–1975 border clashes, visited Mali in his new capacity as the president of Upper Volta. He and President Traoré agreed to submit their dispute to the International Court of Justice at the Hague, which they did. This rapprochement was brokered between the two countries by Algeria, which was seeking to form an Algerian axis in West Africa with which to isolate Morocco and strengthen the POLISARIO. The following month, President Traoré paid an official visit to Upper Volta.

It appeared that the dispute was on its way to a diplomatic solution, a belief reinforced by President Traoré's radio address of October 1985, in which he stressed that taking the dispute to the court would be helpful to regional cooperation. Both sides attach to the area what outside observers consider excessive importance. The region is well watered the year round and provides excellent grazing for livestock, critical resources in the fragile agrarian economies on both sides of the border, especially in the dry season. The assumption that the region may contain mineral wealth (there are no studies or data to support this) plus national pride also impeded attempts to resolve the issue. Thus, moving the dispute to the International Court was seen by most observers as a very positive sign.

The situation deteriorated in early December 1985, when the Malians claimed that Burkina Faso officials attempted to conduct a census in the disputed district, which Mali considered at the time was its own. There are far-reaching implications to census taking: It is both a declaration of sovereignty over an area and a preliminary step in establishing national tax rolls. Mali also claimed that Burkina Faso had sent troops into the disputed area and that diplomacy by Mali and third parties, including the West African Non-Aggression and Defense Accord (ANAD) had failed to produce a withdrawal.[8] With the failure of these efforts, Mali's armed forces moved into the disputed territory on December 25, 1985. In so doing, they took the Burkinabe (people of Burkina Faso) by surprise, as many of the latter, including the president, are Christians and were celebrating Christmas. Unlike the 1974–1975 conflict, which was limited to the disputed territory, this "Christmas War" was spread out over a long expanse of the common frontier.

The military stratagems consisted of occupation of one another's territories, hit-and-run attacks on the ground, and air raids. On December 25, Mali carried out air raids on two large towns in northern Burkina Faso near the border, Djibo and Ouahigouya. Burkina Faso retaliated with an air raid on Sikasso on December 26, in which four Malian civilians were killed and four injured. The Malians quickly recaptured four towns in the disputed area (Dioulouna, Selba, Kouna, and Douna), but the Burkina Faso army raided Zegoua, Mali's southernmost post on the main road between it and Ivory Coast, several hundred kilometers from the disputed territory. Fifteen Malian soldiers were killed there and two military targets destroyed, according to Burkina Faso.

Attempts on the part of third parties at bringing about a cease-fire began almost immediately. The first was worked out by Libyan Foreign Minister Ali Abdussalam al-Treiki in conjunction with Nigeria. A second effort was headed by Abdou Diouf, president of Senegal and chairman of the Organization of African Unity, in conjunction with Félix Houphouet-Boigny, president of Ivory Coast, Gnassingbe Eyadema, president of Togo, Mathieu Kérékou, president of Benin, and Seyni Kountché, president of Niger. Mali and Burkina Faso agreed to end hostilities at midnight on December 27, but the truce was immediately broken. The Malian army attacked Koloko, a small village and frontier post inside of Burkina Faso just across the border, adjacent to the region of Sikasso. The Malians acknowledged that one of their soldiers was killed and eight injured. Mali's air force also raided four major towns inside of

Burkina Faso, Ouahigouya, Djibo, Dédougou, and Tougan, in retaliation for the air strike on Sikasso. The UDPM claimed that the raids caused much property damage and many deaths: All four towns are constructed primarily of mud brick and consist of single-story dwellings.

On December 30, both Mali and Burkina Faso agreed to a cease-fire. The National Council of the Revolution in Burkina Faso publicly assented to the truce worked out by the foreign ministers of seven West African nations—Burkina Faso, Mali, Ivory Coast, Mauritania, Niger, Togo, and Benin, all signers of ANAD. Mali publicly stated it was observing the cease-fire arranged by Libya and Nigeria earlier. This caused concern in other West African countries because that accord called for the inclusion of both countries in a military observer force. International Red Cross representatives were given access to prisoners on both sides, and on January 4, 1986, President Sankara of Burkina Faso presented combat decorations and displayed several captured armored vehicles.

Mali and Burkina Faso finally accepted the truce worked out by ANAD, and peace was formalized by a summit meeting of ANAD leaders at Yamoussoukro, Ivory Coast, later in January 1986.[9] Presidents Sankara and Traoré met and agreed to observe a cease-fire and free prisoners. They also reconfirmed their commitment to abide by the ruling of the International Court of Justice. At the time of the meeting, Sankara had already pulled back his troops, whereas Malian troops were still some 6 miles inside of Burkina Faso.

In their opening arguments before the court in June 1986, the Burkinabe were highly accusatory, telling the court that the Malians were jeopardizing peace in the area by amassing MIG aircraft and tanks. The head of the Malian delegation, Lt. Col. Abdourahmane Maiga, minister of territorial administration and development, spoke of Mali's "good will and desire for peace and dialogue." The Malians were represented before the court by Jean Salmon, professor at the Free University of Brussels, who said that the Malian side had abandoned its ethnic argument used for more than ten years to justify Malian appropriation of the territory. "We are better informed now," he added.[10] These were major concessions on the part of the Malians, who had come under pressure from a variety of sources to take the high ground in settling the dispute. Burkina Faso's revolutionary government of the time was not susceptible to such pressures.

Tensions continued for some time between the two countries, each exchanging accusations about violations of both the spirit and the letter of the Yamoussoukro agreement. However, by December 1986, relations began to improve with the arrival in Ouagadougou of a high-level Malian delegation headed by Gen. Sékou Ly, Mali's minister of defense.

A few days later, a high-level delegation from Burkina Faso visited Bamako, headed by Leandre Bassole, minister of external relations and cooperation. Bassole informed the Malians that as a gesture of goodwill, Burkina Faso had cancelled all military activity along the common border. Finally, on December 22, 1986, the court handed down its decision, giving Burkina Faso the eastern part of the disputed territory and Mali the western part. Both President Traoré and President Sankara praised the decision, and since it was reached, both sides have respected it. In ensuing years, relations between the two countries have greatly improved.[11]

RELATIONS WITH THE REST OF AFRICA

The government of President Keita made a concerted effort to project Mali's influence in Africa well beyond the West African region. Even within the latter area, Mali reached out beyond what had been the limiting francophone confines of the colonial era. President Kwame N'Krumah of Ghana, for example, was the first head of state to visit Bamako after independence. During this visit, he and President Keita announced that Mali and Ghana would have a joint parliament. This led to the creation by the three heads of state of the Guinea-Ghana-Mali union in June 1961, a union that never evolved into a practical political entity. In December 1961, President Keita met with N'Krumah and Sékou Touré of Guinea in Conakry, where they jointly denounced the UN's role in the Congo and accused the West of attempting to eject Patrice Lumumba from his leadership position. Mali was quick to request a meeting of the UN Security Council to discuss the situation in Léopoldville.

In February 1961, Mali formally recognized the revolutionary government of Algeria and the government of Antoine Gizenga in Stanleyville, Congo, characterizing the latter as the only legitimate government in the country. Mali went so far as to send Alioune Diakhite as its ambassador to Stanleyville. Mali's good relations with both Algeria and Morocco placed it in a position along with Ethiopia to mediate "the small war of the sands" between the two countries in October 1963.[12]

Mali did not join the Conseil de l'Entente, a grouping of moderate francophone African states headed by Houphouet Boigny of the Ivory Coast, nor the Organisation Commune Africaine et Malagache (OCAM), which attempted to combat the influence of the more radical states within the OAU. However, Mali did join the CEAO, a grouping of Senegal, Mali, Mauritania, the Ivory Coast, and Niger, whose purpose is to promote trade within the grouping. Mali also joined the Economic

President Moussa Traoré assuming the chairmanship of the Organization of African Unity. Left to right: Ide Oumarou, OAU secretary-general; Kenneth Kaunda of Zambia, outgoing chairman; Moussa Traoré; Javier Perez de Cuellar, UN secretary-general. (Photo from *West Africa*, June 6, 1988, p. 1024; reprinted by permission of the West Africa Publishing Co., Ltd.)

Community of West African States (ECOWAS) founded in Lagos, Nigeria, in 1975.

Mali has consistently supported the Soviet-backed government of Angola and the presence of Cuban troops both there and in Ethiopia. Mali has also consistently had a policy of supporting national liberation groups that are progressive in nature and has not resisted the repeated attempts of Angola, Algeria, and Cuba to push the Third World bloc into the Socialist camp. Mali's attempts to establish closer relations with other African countries geographically far removed from its own borders have been less than successful, primarily because ongoing mutual economic interests are lacking. President Julius Nyerere of Tanzania visited Mali in 1965, and in 1984 President Traoré of Mali paid official visits to Tanzania, Burundi, and Egypt. Mali and Tanzania have always had a sense of solidarity with one another because of their similar political ideologies. However, trade between them is virtually nonexistent.

Although Mali has had limited success in projecting itself as a major influence throughout Africa, individual Malians have occupied important leadership positions in a number of international organizations. Of great significance was President Traoré's assumption of the chairmanship of the OAU in 1988. This was an important milestone for Mali, which for so long has tried to break out from its regional confinement onto the larger African scene. A former Malian minister of health and social affairs, Ali Cissé, became the secretary-general of CILSS, which is headquartered in Ouagadougou, Burkina Faso, and Dr. Cheick Sow, a former Malian director-general of public health, served for many years as secretary-general of OCCGE, a regional health organization of francophone countries with headquarters in Bobo-Dioulasso, Burkina Faso. Louis Nègre, a former Malian minister of finance who negotiated Mali's financial accords with the French in the mid-1960s, became vice president of the African Development Bank in 1970, and assistant UN secretary-general in charge of personnel in 1982. Malian Driss Keita served as secretary-general of the CEAO but was removed in March 1985 at the request of Burkinabe leaders for denigrating their revolution. Another Malian who occupied an important position in the CEAO was Moussa Diakité, who served as director of the organization's Solidarity Fund. The October 27–29, 1984, summit meeting of the CEAO in Bamako was clouded by the alleged embezzlement of community funds by him and two other high-ranking officials. The central figure in the embezzlement scheme was Mohamed Diawara, a former Ivorian cabinet minister who could not account for $13.6 million destined for regional projects. Also implicated was Moussa N'Gom of Senegal. Thomas Sankara, who was then the newly elected president of the CEAO, sharply denounced the embezzlers and promised that they would be swiftly tried in Ouagadougou. The arrest of Moussa Diakité and his dismissal from his post during the Bamako CEAO summit was an acute embarrassment for Mali, as was Sankara's forcing Driss Keita out of the position of secretary-general.[13]

EAST-WEST RELATIONS

Mali has always had a flexible foreign policy, based on promoting its vital interests and on solidarity with socialist political regimes. Although Mali has always maintained that it is nonaligned, its actions in terms of official pronouncements in the press and over the radio and its positions in the UN and other international bodies have more often than not brought it down on the side of the Eastern bloc. Nevertheless, Mali has been deft enough to maintain friendly relations with Western countries, such as the United States, and in so doing, benefit from a broad range of economic and development programs. In this regard, Mali has profited from Western philanthropic traditions that promote assistance regardless of the political ideology of the recipient.

Soon after independence, Mali forged ahead with strengthening its ties to the Eastern bloc. Before 1960 was out, Mali had signed cooperation agreements with the PRC, Yugoslavia, and the Soviet Union, and soon thereafter entered into agreements with Poland, Czechoslovakia, Bulgaria, and North Korea. President Tito of Yugoslavia paid an official visit to Mali in March 1961, and three months later President Keita traveled to Yugoslavia, where he met Tito at Brioni. In September 1961, Keita participated in the Conference of Nonaligned Nations, and six months later he received an official visit from Anastas Mikoyan, first vice president of the Soviet Union. During 1962, Keita visited Moscow and Prague and also Washington, D.C. He made another visit to the Soviet Union in 1965.[14]

President Keita also moved ahead quickly in establishing diplomatic relations with the PRC. In January 1963, Chou En-lai, China's foreign minister, visited Bamako, and the following year President Keita visited China, where he issued a communiqué stating, "The situation is very favorable for a revolution throughout Africa." Although he denounced U.S. atomic weapons testing, with reference to the first Chinese atomic explosion, Keita said, "This bomb is the bomb of peace." China's Marshal Chen-Yi, minister of foreign affairs, visited Bamako in September 1965, and the following year China agreed to provide Mali with a broad range of technical and economic assistance, including the construction of a powerful radio transmitter.

Che Guevara, the Cuban minister of industry, visited Bamako in January 1965. Other high-ranking emissaries from North Vietnam, North Korea, and the Eastern bloc continued to visit Bamako, bringing with them modest loans, development programs, material and technical expertise. The Soviets supplied Mali with military weapons and equipment and assistance in mineral exploration, and the Chinese constructed three factories for the production of cigarettes, matches, and textiles. In addition, both the Soviets and the Chinese provided medical personnel, and the latter also sent agricultural experts to assist in the development of the Office du Niger. Smaller Eastern bloc countries such as Bulgaria and Poland established embassies in Bamako and provided very modest assistance in return for trade advantages and windfall propaganda for their help. These two countries closed their embassies in Bamako in the 1970s in an economy move but still maintain diplomatic relations with Mali.

During the Vietnam War, Mali's sympathies were with North Vietnam, which at the time maintained an embassy in Bamako. Mali was strident in its condemnation of the U.S. role in Vietnam and in Korea as well. Thus, although President Keita claimed that his government was nonaligned, it clearly was not, either in rhetoric or in practice.

By the mid-1960s, Mali had thirteen embassies abroad, in addition to offices at a number of international organizations. Of the embassies, a significant number were situated in Communist bloc countries, including North Vietnam, North Korea, the PRC, the Soviet Union, Yugoslavia,

East Germany, and Cuba. Some forty-seven countries maintained diplomatic relations with Mali, but only twenty-two opened embassies in Bamako. Of these, ten belonged to socialist or Communist countries. By the time of the coup d'état of 1968, Mali clearly was in the socialist camp, despite its claims of nonalignment. In 1987, Bamako still had twenty-two foreign embassies. However, by this time, Bulgaria, Ghana, Israel, and Poland had closed theirs; they were replaced by those of Iran, Iraq, Libya, and Malaysia. The former two were opened in the interests of promoting solidarity with their position in the Iran-Iraq War.

The government of President Traoré has maintained a certain commitment to the foreign policy of the Keita government, but with significant exceptions. Its foreign policy has been pragmatic and has aimed at maintaining an equidistance between East and West and between China and the Soviet Union. Mali's increasing reliance on the West and on Western institutions such as the World Bank and the International Monetary Fund has necessitated an abandonment of useless anti-Western rhetoric and promoted closer ties with the West. However, it has not forced Mali to abandon its long-standing relationships with the Eastern bloc, which over time have lost much of their practical value, except for those with China and the Soviet Union. The Soviet Union still provides Mali with military hardware and assistance in other development projects, and China is a principal importer of Malian goods and sponsors a broad range of assistance programs, including one to halt the spread of the desert in the north. President Traoré has paid official visits to both the Soviet Union and China, and on a 1986 trip he also went to North Korea. High-level delegations from the Eastern bloc and China have regularly visited Mali in recent years, emphasizing the friendly relations that still exist.

Mali has maintained friendly relations with Saudi Arabia in part because of the large number of Malians who annually make the pilgrimage to Mecca. Saudi Arabia has provided Mali with substantial assistance in the form of direct aid and through larger international Arab bodies such as the Arab Bank for Economic Development in Africa and the OPEC Fund for International Development. Mali has made a conscious effort to strike neutral ground between the conservative and radical factions in the Arab world. This explains Mali's relations with Saudi Arabia, Egypt, Tunisia, and Morocco on the one hand, and with Algeria, Libya, and the PLO on the other. President Traoré visited Egypt in 1984 and Tunisia in 1986.

For a long time, Mali was able to balance its relations with the Arabs and with Israel. In 1960, Mali signed three cooperation agreements with Israel, signaling the beginning of a cordial relationship that was to last until diplomatic relations were broken in 1973 as a result of the

Yom Kippur War. Mali had little choice in the matter of severing diplomatic relations with Israel; it was forced to do so out of solidarity with Arab members of the OAU. During the time that Mali maintained diplomatic relations with Israel, the latter provided technical assistance in a number of areas. Some Malians privately admire and identify with Israel because it is a small country surrounded by numerous enemies, yet one that has managed to achieve stunning military victories over them while at the same time making impressive gains in development.

Mali has maintained friendly relations with the two Germanys, receiving substantial assistance from both. The Federal Republic is a major trading partner, consuming 15 percent of Mali's exports and providing about the same in imports. In addition, it has given Mali significant loans and grants, transforming some of the former at later dates into outright gifts. The German Democratic Republic has supported a number of agricultural development projects, notably a model farm at Seno in central Mali.

RELATIONS WITH THE UNITED STATES

Immediately after its independence, Mali commanded special interest from U.S. administrations because of its close ties with Eastern bloc countries and its socialist form of government. As in neighboring Guinea, the aim of U.S. foreign policy was to maintain correct relations with Mali and a presence there in order to offset to some degree the overwhelming influence of Communist countries, especially the Soviet Union and China. In a sense, the Malians were willing pawns in this exercise of East-West rivalry, as they economically benefited from both sides.

During most of the 1960s, Mali aligned itself solidly with North Vietnam and spewed forth anti-American diatribes over Radio Mali and laced its official newspaper, *L'Essor*, with anti-American invectives. This rhetoric was not confined to the war in Vietnam, but extended to many aspects of U.S. political, social, and economic life. The United States was consistently portrayed to the Malian public as an imperialist and neocolonialist nation where crime, racism, and poverty were rampant. Most of the copy for these diatribes in the mass media was supplied by Communist news agencies, although some was written in Bamako.

American embassy staff in Bamako and U.S. aid workers were regularly subjected to a steady barrage of petty harassments and treated by many Malian officials with hostility. Severe travel restrictions were placed on U.S. nationals, who could not journey outside of the Bamako area without written permission.[15] Anti-American sentiment was heightened during President Modibo Keita's Cultural Revolution, a time when

U.S. foreign aid to Mali was significantly reduced, although that occurred, not because of increased tensions between the United States and Mali, but because of a policy change of the Nixon administration concerning aid to Africa.

Following the coup d'état of 1968, the steady barrage of anti-American rhetoric abated. However, it continued to surface with significant frequency into the early 1970s. This was due to the presence of radical revolutionaries in the state-run press and media services and Mali's continued economic dependence and close political ties with the Eastern bloc. Eventually, the shrill rhetoric disappeared in the 1970s, replaced by an absence of comment either negative or positive about the United States. This was a concession to the Communist bloc, on which Mali still heavily depended.

The U.S. role in Mali's development has always been significant, although during the Keita regime and the early years of military rule, it was rarely publicly recognized. U.S. aid has come in the form of loans, grants, and the provision of technical advisers for a broad range of projects in health, industry, commerce, education, and agriculture. During the droughts of the 1970s and 1980s, the United States provided Mali with massive relief in the form of grain shipments and also launched a variety of development programs aimed at long-term solutions. This aid saved many Malians from starvation. The total value of U.S. aid to Mali between 1961 and mid-1988 amounted to $350 million.

During the 1970s, President Traoré frequently expressed a desire to visit the United States. However, no invitation was extended, given Mali's continued close ties with the Communist bloc and the concerns of the U.S. Department of State that inviting him would antagonize Upper Volta.[16] President Traoré's pragmatic politics brought Mali closer to the West during most of the 1980s. This led to the adoption of new free-enterprise economic policies while Mali continued to express its views on international problems as a nonaligned state. Economic necessity and political survival forced Traoré's government to make positive steps toward bettering relations with the West, including the United States. As a sign of these improved relations, then–Vice President George Bush visited Mali for several hours on March 10, 1985, for the purpose of presenting the government with a $24.6 million assistance program to encourage free-market agricultural practices. This was the highest level visit ever paid to Mali by a U.S. official and indicated how much U.S.-Mali relations had improved during the 1980s.[17] The resolution of the border dispute between Mali and Burkina Faso in December 1986 removed a major obstacle to a U.S. visit by President Traoré. Still, he was not invited.

In early 1988, President Traoré assumed the chairmanship of the OAU. During the following months, the United States made significant progress in its mediation efforts to resolve the war in Angola and to facilitate the independence of Namibia, bringing together the South Africans, Angolans, and Cubans at a series of direct meetings. President Traoré was finally invited to Washington by the Reagan administration. Although administration officials saw his visit as representing better relations between the two countries, they also viewed it as an OAU endorsement of then current U.S.-led talks on Angola and Namibia. The Malians, for their part, regarded the invitation as recognition of Mali's stability and free-market initiatives and of the OAU's role in mediating Africa's major political problems.

The Reagan administration had given a low rating to the OAU in the early 1980s when it was strongly influenced by radical leaders such as Lt. Col. Mengistu Haile Mariam of Ethiopia and Colonel Qaddafi. However, the administration saw an improvement in the OAU in the late 1980s and a potential useful role for it in its mediation plans in southern Africa. Thus, when President Traoré made his first official visit to the United States October 6–9, 1988, he was welcomed not only as the president of Mali but also as the chairman of the OAU.

During the eight years that President Reagan was in office, President Traoré was only the second African head of state ever to be honored with the pomp and ceremony of a South Lawn arrival and a White House state dinner.[18] In his welcoming address at the White House and in his private talks, President Reagan expressed appreciation for the role that President Traoré had played in foreign affairs, particularly in regard to Southern Africa, the western Sahara, and the conflict between Chad and Libya. President Reagan praised highly President Traoré's efforts to resolve Africa's regional conflicts and observed that Mali and the United States enjoy close and cordial relations. For his part, President Traoré stressed Mali's concerns over the Chad-Libya conflict, the African debt problem, and U.S.-Mali bilateral relations.

The visit was a great success from the perspectives of both sides. The United States obtained the moral endorsement of the OAU for its Southern African talks, and Mali solidified its bilateral relations with the United States and was given an opportunity to solicit private-sector U.S. investment. The Malian mass media emphasized not only Traoré's U.S. program but also his meetings as OAU chairman in New York with diverse world leaders such as Javier Perez de Cuellar, secretary-general of the UN, U.S. Secretary of State George Shultz, and POLISARIO minister of foreign affairs, Abbas Moustapha. As chairman of the OAU, Traoré spoke before the UN General Assembly, emphasizing the problems of African debt, toxic wastes, refugees, and South Africa.

Long-time Mali observers in the United States found President Traoré's words and actions a far cry from those of his predecessor and of his own government during the 1970s. There is a famous Bambara proverb often recited in Mali that says: *Jiri kuru mè omè ji la a te kè bamayé*—no matter how long a log remains in water, it can never become a crocodile. The wisdom of this proverb will be proven wrong if socialist Mali is able to transform itself into a free-enterprise state. Only time will tell. Meanwhile, on his return to Mali, President Traoré created a commission to follow up on the progress made in U.S.-Mali relations, which he said, "should be fruitful from now on."

Notes

Notes to Chapter 1

1. Mali's official name is la République du Mali, and French is the official language. The Malian flag is a tricolor, consisting of three vertical bands, green, yellow, and red. The country's motto is Un Peuple—Un But—Une Foi (One people—one goal—one faith).

2. For details of these border and name changes, see Pascal James Imperato and Eleanor M. Imperato, *Mali: A Handbook of Historical Statistics*, Boston, G. K. Hall, 1982, pp. 1–2.

3. Réné Chudeau, "Le plateau Mandingue," *Annales de Géographie* 30:362–373, 1921.

4. Suzanne DaVeau, *Recherches morphologiques sur la région de Bandiagara*, Dakar, IFAN, 1959.

5. One of the earliest and most extensive descriptions of the Hombori Mountains and the Bandiagara Cliffs was given by Louis Desplagnes in his book, *Le Plateau Central Nigérien*, Paris, Larose, 1910.

6. The most detailed geographic and ethnographic study of the Inland Delta of the Niger is Jean Gallais's *Le delta intérieur du Niger. Etude de géographie régionale*, vols. 1 and 2, Dakar, IFAN, 1967.

7. The Manantali Dam was constructed as part of a development scheme for the Senegal River Basin sponsored by the Organisation pour la Mise-en-valeur du Fleuve Sénégal (OMVS). Another dam, the Diama Dam, was constructed near the mouth of the river in Senegal. See John Montague, "Miracle or White Elephant? *West Africa*, March 31, 1986, pp. 666–667, and John Walsh, "A Project Born of Hope, Desperation," *Science* 232:1081–1083, 1986, for the controversy concerning both projects.

8. Periodic droughts have been the rule in Mali. See Derek Winstanley, "Climate Changes and the Future of the Sahel," in Michael H. Glantz (ed.), *The Politics of Natural Disaster: The Case of the Sahel Drought*, New York, Praeger, 1976, pp. 282–302.

9. A graphic description of the famine associated with the 1916–1917 drought is given by Fily Dabo Sissoko in his *La savanne rouge*, Avignon, Presses Universelles, 1962, p. 36.

149

10. Deforestation around urban centers due to tree cutting for fuel has become a serious problem in Mali. In the 1960s, firewood for Bamako was gathered 10 miles away. Today, people must get it from 100 miles away. In 1987, Mali enacted legislation requiring household use of efficient fuel-conserving stoves and established a force of "stove police" to enforce it. See James Brooke, "Fight to Save African Forests Turns to Stoves," *New York Times*, March 20, 1988, p. 20.

11. For a detailed account of Mali's wildlife, see Imperato and Imperato, *Mali*, pp. 183–185.

12. K. Koch, "Dramatizing the Plight of West African Wildlife," *Christian Science Monitor*, October 19, 1987, p. 16.

13. *Population Growth and Policies in Sub-Saharan Africa*, Washington, D.C., World Bank, 1986, p. 88.

14. For a detailed description of Mali's various ethnic groups, see Bokar N'Diaye, *Groupes ethniques au Mali*, Bamako, Editions Populaires, 1970.

Notes to Chapter 2

1. Marcellin Boule and Henri Vallois, *L'homme d'Asselar (Sahara)*, Paris, Masson, 1932.

2. Henri Lhote, "Oases of Art in the Sahara," *National Geographic* 172:181–191, 1987.

3. J. D. Clark, "The Spread of Food Production in sub-Saharan Africa," *Journal of African History* 3:211–228, 1962.

4. The term *Western Sudan* is used to describe the area south of the Sahara that includes the Sahel and the savanna country from Senegal east to Niger. The word *Sudan* comes from the Arabic, *bilad es sudan*, "land of the black people."

5. Nehemia Levtzion, *Ancient Ghana and Mali*, London, Methuen, 1973, p. 14.

6. Susan K. McIntosh and Roderick J. McIntosh, *Prehistoric Investigations in the Region of Jenne, Mali: A Study of the Development of Urbanism in the Sahel*, Oxford, Cambridge Monographs in African Archaeology, No. 2, *British Archaeological Reports*, 2 vols., 1980.

7. Susan K. McIntosh and Roderick J. McIntosh, "Finding West Africa's Oldest City," *National Geographic* 162:396–418, 1982.

8. Bernard de Grunne, *Terres Cuites Anciennes de l'Ouest Africain: Ancient Terracottas from West Africa*. Louvain-la-Neuve, Université Catholique de Louvain, 1980.

9. Nehemia Levtzion, "The Sahara and the Sudan from the Arab Conquest of the Maghreb to the Rise of the Almoravids," in J. D. Fage (ed.), *The Cambridge History of Africa*, vol. 2, Cambridge, Cambridge University Press, 1978, pp. 637–684.

10. See Levtzion, *Ancient Ghana and Mali*, pp. 16–28.

11. Nehemia Levtzion, "The Western Maghreb and Sudan," in Roland Oliver (ed.), *The Cambridge History of Africa*, vol. 3, Cambridge, Cambridge University Press, 1977, pp. 331–462.

12. Raymond Mauny and Paul Thomassey, "Campagne de fouilles à Koumbi-Saleh," *Bulletin de IFAN* 13:438–462, 1951.

13. See E. W. Bovill, *The Golden Trade of the Moors*, London, Oxford University Press, 1958, pp. 66–85.

14. See Nehemia Levtzion and J. F. Hopkins, *Corpus of Early Arabic Sources for West African History*, New York, Cambridge University Press, 1981.

15. For the oral traditions about Soundiata Keita, see Djibril Tamsir Niane, *Sundiata: An Epic of Old Mali*, trans. G. D. Pickett, London, Longmans, 1965.

16. A full discussion of these events is given in Levtzion, *Ancient Ghana and Mali*, pp. 66–72, and in Levtzion, "The Western Maghreb and the Sudan," pp. 376–396.

17. See Ross E. Dunn, *The Adventures of Ibn Battuta. A Muslim Traveler of the Fourteenth Century*, Berkeley, University of California Press, 1987.

18. Leo Africanus was captured in 1518 by Christian Corsairs and presented to Pope Leo X, a Medici pope. He was freed, given a pension, converted to Christianity, and taught Arabic at the University of Bologna. His name, El-Hassan Ibn Wezaz, was changed to John Leo, and he became known as Leo Africanus. In 1526, he completed his book, *The History and Description of Africa and the Notable Things Therein Contained*. It was published in Italian in 1550 and in English in 1660.

19. Es Sadi is credited with writing the *Tarikh-es-Sudan*, a history of the Western Sudan whose major focus is on the Songhay Empire. A slightly earlier history, *Tarikh-el-Fettach*, is generally credited to Mohammed Kati (1468–?), a Timbuctoo scholar. It also focuses on Songhay but contains important information on Ghana and Mali.

20. Detailed histories of Songhay are contained in both the *Tarikh-el-Fettach* and the *Tarikh-es-Sudan.*

21. Leo Africanus traveled through Songhay in 1510 during the reign of Askia Mohammed. The account of his voyage, first published in Italian in 1550, represents one of the most important descriptions of Songhay. See Leo Africanus, *History and Description of Africa*, 3 vols. London, Hakluyt Society, 1896.

22. See J. O. Hunwick, "Songhay, Borno and Hausaland in the Sixteenth Century," in J.F.A. Ajayi and Michael Crowder (eds.), *History of West Africa*, vol. 1, New York, Columbia University Press, 1976, pp. 264–301.

23. For an overview of the Moroccan invasion, see Bovill, *The Golden Trade of the Moors*, pp. 134–178.

24. See Michel Abitol, *Tombouctou et les Arma*, Paris, Maisonneuve et Larose, 1979, for details on the decline of the Pashalik, pp. 221–243.

25. Ibid., pp. 66–67. The *Tarikh-el-Fettach* gives graphic details about the Moroccan treatment of Timbuctoo's scholars.

26. See Elias N. Saad, *Social History of Timbuctoo*, Cambridge, Cambridge University Press, 1983, for the role of scholars in Timbuctoo's life and history.

27. Ibid., p. 46.

28. Leo Africanus gave a detailed description of imports and exports in the Western Sudan in the sixteenth century. See Leo Africanus, *History and Description of Africa*, vol. 1, pp. 123–128, pp. 173–174; vol. 2, p. 309; vol. 3, pp. 819–834.

29. For descriptions of Djénné's social, commercial, and political history, see Charles Montiel, *Une Cité soudanaise, Djénné, métropole du delta central du Niger*, Paris, Société d'Editions Géographiques, Maritime et Coloniales, 1932, 2nd ed., London, International African Institute, 1971.

30. For a detailed history of the Bambara, see Louis Tauxier, *Histoire des Bambara*, Paris, Librairie Orientaliste Paul Geuthner, 1942.

31. See Amadou Hampaté Ba and Jacques Daget, *L'Empire Peul du Macina*, vol. 1, 1818–1853, Paris, Mouton, 1962.

32. The Qadiriya brotherhood is an Islamic mystical order that originated in Baghdad with Sidi Abu-el-Qader (1079–1166). It became popular in West Africa in the late fifteenth and early sixteenth centuries. The Tijaniya brotherhood is an Islamic mystical order founded in Fez, Morocco, by Ahmad el Tijani (1737–1815). The founders of Islamic mystical orders, also known as Sufi orders, are usually venerated by their followers.

33. For the history of Tall's jihad, see David Robinson, *The Holy War of Umar Tal: The Western Sudan in the Mid-Nineteenth Century*, Oxford, Oxford University Press, 1985.

34. Amadou Tall's empire is described in detail in B. O. Oloruntimehin, *The Segu Tukulor Empire*, London, Longmans, 1972.

35. A detailed study of Samory Touré is Yves Person, *Samori: Une Revolution Dyula*, 2 vols., Dakar, IFAN, 1968.

36. For a discussion of the balance between Islam and Bambara interests, see John Ralph Willis, "The Western Sudan from the Moroccan Invasion (1591) to the Death of Al-Mukhtar Al-Kunti (1811)," in Ajayi and Crowder, *History of West Africa*, vol. 1, pp. 544–545.

Notes to Chapter 3

1. Details on the explorers who reached Timbuctoo are contained in Brian Gardner, *The Quest for Timbuctoo*, New York, William Morrow, 1939.

2. An excellent account of France's diplomatic and military activities in the Western Sudan is found in A. S. Kanya-Forstner, *The Conquest of the Western Sudan: A Study in French Military Imperialism*, Cambridge, Cambridge University Press, 1969.

3. A French colonial view of the exploration and military acquisition of what is now Mali is found in Jacques Méniaud's *Les Pionniers du Soudan avant, et après Archinard (1879–1894)*, 2 vols., Paris, Société des Publications Modernes, 1931.

4. For details on French West Africa, see *French West Africa* vol. 1, *The Federation*, London, Naval Intelligence Division, 1943. Details about French colonial administration in West Africa are found in Robert Delavignette, *Freedom and Authority in French West Africa*, Oxford, Oxford University Press, 1950.

5. An excellent description of William Ponty's life and career is given by G. Wesley Johnson, "William Ponty and Republican Paternalism in French West Africa (1866–1915)," in L. H. Gann and Peter Duignan (eds.), *African Proconsuls: European Governors in Africa*, New York, The Free Press, 1978, pp. 127–156.

6. See Keletiqui Mariko, *Les Touaregs Oulleminden*, Paris, Karthala, 1984, for specifics on the Tuareg revolt.

7. See Issa Baba Traoré, *Koumi Diossé*, Bamako, Editions Populaires, 1962.

8. The Hamallist movement is described in detail in Louis Brenner, *West African Sufi: The Religious Heritage and Spiritual Search of Cerno Bokar Saalif Taal*, Berkeley, University of California Press, 1984.

9. The strike on the Dakar-Niger railroad is presented in fictional form in Ousmane Sembene, *Les Bouts de bois de dieu* (God's bits of wood), Paris, Presses Pocket, 1960.

10. See Frank Snyder, *One-Party Government in Mali: Transition Toward Control*, New Haven and London, Yale University Press, 1965, pp. 9–35.

11. See Thomas Hodgkin, *Nationalism in Colonial Africa*, New York, New York University Press, 1957, pp. 63–83, 84–93, for a discussion of new urban agglomerations and of voluntary associations.

12. See Snyder, *One-Party Government in Mali*, pp. 36–61.

13. See Philippe Decraene, *Le Mali*, Paris, Presses Universitaires de France, 1980, pp. 55–65.

14. For the history of the Mali Federation, see William J. Foltz, *From French West Africa to the Mali Federation*, New Haven and London, Yale University Press, 1965.

Notes to Chapter 4

1. For details of Mali's 1977 local administrative reforms, see Pascal James Imperato and Eleanor M. Imperato, *Mali: A Handbook of Historical Statistics*, Boston, G. K. Hall, 1982, pp. 6–8.

2. Fily Dabo Sissoko's political career is presented in detail by Paule Brasseur, "Le baton et le caiman, ou Fily Dabo Sissoko et la France," in *Etudes Africaines Offerts à Henri Brunschwig*, Paris, EHESI, 1981, pp. 399–409.

3. For a first-hand account of Mali's 1968 coup d'état, see Pascal James Imperato, *A Wind in Africa: A Story of Modern Medicine in Mali*, St. Louis, Warren H. Green, 1975, pp. 244–256.

4. Policy issues were regularly debated within the CMLN at its weekly meeting. On a number of occasions, differences of opinion were so strong that they resulted in fisticuffs among members.

5. Captain Diby Silas Diarra was a highly feared martinet who combined exceptional administrative abilities with cruelty and ruthlessness. He personally put down the rebellion of the Tuareg in the Adrar des Iforas in the early 1960s, using brutal and inhumane methods. As commandant of the *cercle* of Kidal, he was in charge of the penitentiary, where political prisoners were held under abominable conditions. The CMLN made him governor of the Gao region and later governor of the Mopti region. His arrest on charges of planning a coup d'état may have been preemptive on the part of the CMLN. Diarra's brutality toward the Tuareg is discussed by Keletiqui Mariko, *Les Touaregs Ouelleminden*, Paris, Karthala, 1984, pp. 109–110.

6. An incisive analysis of the inner workings of the CMLN is provided by David P. Rawson, "Mali: Soldiers as Politicians," in Isaac James Mowoe (ed.),

The Performance of Soldiers as Governors: African Politics and the African Military, Washington, D.C., University Press of America, 1980, pp. 265–312.

7. For the organizational structure of the UDPM, see Valerie Sanford Griffith, "Republic of Mali," in *World Encyclopedia of Political Systems and Parties,* vol. 1, ed. George E. De Lury, New York, Facts on File Publications, 1983, pp. 662–663.

8. It was also rumored that the president's personal physician, Faran Samaké, played a role in Keita's death. Shortly after Keita's death, Samaké died under mysterious circumstances. It was rumored that he had committed suicide, but some government officials claimed he died from an asthma attack.

9. See Rawson, "Mali: Soldiers as Politicians," for details on the arrest of Doukara and Bagayoko.

10. See Tikum Mbah Azonga, "Traore Paves the Way," *West Africa,* July 21, 1986, p. 1519, for specifics of the 1986 ministerial changes.

11. See "Kamikaze Minister Leaves His Mark in Bamako," *Africa Report* 30:6, 1987.

12. For a summary of the third regular UDPM party congress, see "Conclusions from Bamako," *West Africa,* May 16, 1988, p. 876.

13. President Traoré emphasized these points in an after-lunch speech he gave at the U.S. Department of State, Washington, D.C., on October 6, 1988 (personal observation).

Notes to Chapter 5

1. "Dateline, Mali," *West Africa,* May 30, 1988, p. 997.

2. See Bokar N'Diaye, *Groupes ethniques au Mali,* Bamako, Editions Populaires, 1970, for a comprehensive coverage of Mali's ethnic groups.

3. For a description of the Keita government's brutal treatment of the Tuareg, see Keletiqui Mariko, *Les Touaregs Ouelleminden,* Paris, Karthala, 1984, pp. 109–110.

4. A great deal of drought aid was misappropriated. Kissima Doukara, who headed Mali's drought relief efforts, was convicted in March 1979 of embezzling $9 million in drought-related aid.

5. For a detailed account of the Hamalliya, see Louis Brenner, *West African Sufi: The Religious Heritage and Spiritual Search of Cerno Bokar Saalif Taal,* Berkeley, University of California Press, 1984.

6. The history of the Wahabiya in Mali is covered by Lansiné Kaba in *The Wahhabiyya: Islamic Reform and Politics in French West Africa,* Evanston, Ill., Northwestern University Press, 1974.

7. "Islamic Centre," *West Africa,* May 4, 1987, p. 891.

8. Both the Roman Catholic church and the Protestant denominations have made special efforts to Africanize their clergy.

9. See Dominique Zahan, *The Bambara,* Leiden, E. J. Brill, 1974, pp. 1–9.

10. See "Mali," in *International Handbook of Universities,* 10th ed., ed. D. J. Actken and Ann C.M. Taylor, New York, Stockton Press, 1986.

11. "Cabinet Shuffle," *West Africa,* June 16, 1986, p. 1289.

12. See Pascal James Imperato, "The Role of Women in Traditional Healing Among the Bambara of Mali," *Transactions of the Royal Society of Tropical Medicine and Hygiene* 76:766–770, 1981.

13. M. T. Abela de la Rivière, "Les Sarakole du Mali et leur emigration en France," *Etudes Maliennes* 7:1–12, 1973.

14. See Guy Belloncle, *Jeunes Ruraux du Sahel: Une expérience de formation de jeunes alphabetisés au Mali,* Paris, Librairie-Editions Harmattan, 1979.

15. Personal communication, Benitieni Fofana, minister of health and social affairs, Bamako, January 1973.

16. For details of Salif Keita's life and career, see Kwabena Fosu-Mensah, "The Mansa of Mali," *West Africa*, August 24, 1987, pp. 1636–1637.

17. For details on Salif Keita's U.S. debut, see Daphne Topouzis, "Voices from West Africa: Youssou N'Dour and Salif Keita," *Africa Report* 33,5:66–69, 1988.

18. Non-Malians, particularly French nationals, have written novels set in Mali. See Paule Brasseur, *Bibliographie Générale du Mali,* Dakar, IFAN, 1964, pp. 194–196, for a complete listing up to 1960. Her subsequent volume of the same title, covering 1961–1970 and published in 1974, contains an additional listing on pp. 111–113. The most popular novel published in the 1980s and set in Mali is Maryse Condé's *Segu,* New York, Viking Press, 1987. A native of Guadeloupe, Condé claims to be a descendant of the Bambara of Mali, whom she features in her novel.

19. Details concerning the legal and ethnical issues in the Ououloguem case are presented by Eric Sellin, "Unknown Voice of Yambo Ououloguem," *Yale French Studies: Traditional and African Literature* 53:137–162, 1976.

20. For details on Cissé's life and career, see "Souleymane Cisse," *Afrique Contemporaine* 144:96, 1987, and "Interview with Souleyman Cisse," *West Africa,* December 7, 1987, p. 2378.

21. See "Mali: Call On Youths," *West Africa*, October 10–16, 1988, p. 1922.

22. See Pascal James Imperato, "Modern and Traditional Medicine: The Case of Mali," *Annals of Internal Medicine* 95:650–651, 1981.

23. For details on the USAID-funded Smallpox Eradication–Measles Control Program in Mali, see Pascal James Imperato, *A Wind in Africa: A Story of Modern Medicine in Mali,* St. Louis, Warren H. Green, 1975. For details on the onchocerciasis control program, see *Onchocerciasis Control in the Volta River Basin Area,* Geneva, WHO, 1973.

24. For a history of meningococcal meningitis epidemics in Mali and details on the great 1969–1971 epidemic, see Pascal James Imperato, "Epidemic Meningococcal Meningitis: The Case of Mali," *Bulletin of the New York Academy of Medicine* 59:818–832, 1983, and Pascal James Imperato, *Medical Detective,* New York, Richard Marek, 1979, pp. 107–121.

25. For a description of the health status of famine victims in northern Mali in 1974, see Pascal James Imperato, *Report of a Health and Nutrition Study of the Sahel Relief and Rehabilitation Program in the Republic of Mali,* Washington, D.C., American Public Health Association/USAID, No. 125, 1975, and T. I. Kloth, *Sahel Nutrition Survey 1974,* Atlanta, Ga., Centers for Disease Control, U.S. Public Health Service, 1974.

26. The development of early health services in Mali is described by H. Gallay, *Trois années d'assistance médicales aux indigènes et de lutte contre la variole*, Paris, Larose, 1909.

27. For a comprehensive discussion of Mali's cost-recovery efforts in health care, see "Cost Recovery Policy in Mali," in Ronald J. Vogel, *Cost Recovery in the Health Care Sector. Selected Country Studies in West Africa*, Washington, D.C., The World Bank, 1988, pp. 57–86.

28. Ibid.

29. Ibid.

30. Traditional medicine in Mali is described by Pascal James Imperato, *African Folk Medicine: Practices and Beliefs of the Bambara and Other Peoples*, Baltimore, Md., York Press, 1977.

Notes to Chapter 6

1. For a history of French trading houses in the Sudan, see Jean Charbonneau and Réné Charbonneau, *Marchés et marchands d'Afrique Noire*, Paris, Editions Vieux-Colombier, 1961.

2. The role of western Mali and the town of Kayes in the early commercial and economic life of the colony is dealt with in great detail in Rokiatou N'Diaye Keita, *Kayes et le Haut Sénégal*, vols. 1 and 2, Bamako, Editions Populaires, 1972.

3. An African perspective of the history of the Office du Niger containing details about forced labor and the methods used to settle people in the scheme is provided by Amidu Magasa, *Papa-commandant a jété un grand filet devant nous, les exploités des rives Niger (1902–1962)*, Paris, Maspero, 1978.

4. For a clear description of state-induced disincentives for farmers, see Youssouf Gaye Kébé, "L'agriculture, le paysan, sa terre et l'état," in Pierre Jacquemot (ed.), *Le Mali: Le paysan et l'état*, Paris, Editions l'Harmattan, 1981, pp. 22–102.

5. See Jacques Albert, "La privatisation des entreprises publiques en Afrique noire francophone," *Afrique Contemporaine* 143:35–50, 1987.

6. The multifaceted FAO fisheries project in Mopti is described by André Szabo in *Améliorations Possibles de l'Utilisation des Produits de la Pêche*, Rome, United Nations Food and Agriculture Organization, 1970.

7. A detailed discussion of the problems of Mali's state-run enterprises is given by Moussa Cola Cissé, "Les 'acquis du peuple'; les sociétés et entreprises d'état," in *Le Mali: Le paysan et l'état*, ed. Pierre Jacquemot, Paris, Editions l'Harmattan, 1981, pp. 131–158.

8. See Marvin Howe, "U.S. Visit by Mali Leader Reflects Better Ties," *New York Times*, October 6, 1988, p. A-16.

9. For details on the Malian mass-media coverage of President Traore's 1988 U.S. visit, see "Media Reaction to President Traore's U.S. visit," Unclassified Cable, American Embassy, Bamako, Mali, to U.S. Secretary of State, October 21, 1988, U.S. Information Agency Archives.

10. The problems and concerns relating to the construction of the Manantali and Diama dams are discussed by John Walsh in "A Project Born of Hope, Desperation," *Science* 232:1081–1083, 1986.

11. "Sikamann Buys Gold Concession," *West Africa*, May 23, 1988, p. 934.

12. "Mali," *West Africa*, May 5, 1986, p. 967.

13. In the 1974 crash, forty-seven passengers were killed. The plane, which had a Soviet pilot, ran out of fuel when it was unable to make a scheduled stop in Niamey because of weather conditions. In the 1985 crash, fifty-one passengers were killed, three of them Americans. The crash was caused by an explosion in one of the plane's engines.

14. For a detailed account of U.S. aid to Mali from 1960 through 1988, see "Economic Assistance," Unclassified Cable, American Embassy, Bamako, Mali, to U.S. Secretary of State, October 9, 1988, U.S. Information Agency Archives.

15. Ibid.

16. "IMF Team in Bamako," *West Africa*, August 31, 1937, p. 1705.

17. See Marvin Howe, "U.S. Visit by Mali Leader Reflects Better Ties," for details on the economic objectives of President Traore's 1988 U.S. visit.

Notes to Chapter 7

1. For a description of Mali's early relations with France, see Philippe Decraene, *Le Mali*, Paris, Presses Universitaires de France, 1980, pp. 72–76.

2. A pro-Keita view of the 1967 accords with the French is provided by Cheick Oumar Diarrah, *Le Mali de Modibo Keita*, Paris, Editions l'Harmattan, 1986, pp. 121–128.

3. See "France to Aid Returnees," *West Africa*, January 11, 1988, p. 55.

4. See "Mali-Mauritania Agreement," *West Africa*, February 23, 1963, p. 320.

5. See "Border Talks," *West Africa*, August 10, 1987, p. 1557.

6. See "Talks with Algeria," *West Africa*, December 16, 1986, p. 2627.

7. For details on Colonel Qaddafi's 1985 West African tour, see "Qaddafi Tours West Africa," *West Africa*, December 16, 1985, p. 2668.

8. An excellent overview of the background to the Mali–Burkina Faso border dispute is presented by David Leith Crum in his article, "Mali and the U.M.O.A.: A Case Study of Economic Integration," *Journal of Modern African Studies* 22:469–486, 1984. Segun Johnson in his article, "Burkina-Mali War: Is Nigeria Still a Regional Power?" *India Quarterly*, July-September, 1986, pp. 294–308, cogently argues that Mali's military offensive against Burkina Faso in 1985 was in part a repercussion of President Sankara's close ties with Libya. Mali had become increasingly concerned about the closeness of these ties and Sankara's modeling of his revolution on Libya's, seeing in them a possible threat to its own security. During the months prior to the onset of the conflict, Burkina Faso had subjected Mali to a barrage of provocative rhetoric and in a September 1985 speech, Sankara had said that the Burkinabe revolution was available to anyone. This was interpreted in Mali as a call to Malians to revolt against their government. Thus, Mali may have used what otherwise might have been a minor provocation as an excuse for a military operation aimed at more than just asserting its claim to a stretch of barren territory.

The respective versions of how the 1985 war began is given in "Mali/ Burkina: Two Sides, One Peace," *West Africa*, January 27, 1986, pp. 170–172. Sankara held that Mali used the border dispute as a pretext for all-out war against Burkina's revolution. The Malian government stated that Sankara had in fact appealed to its people to revolt against their government and had sent troops into the disputed area on December 14, the anniversary of the start of the 1974 border clashes. It was the presence of these troops and Burkinabe census taking, the Malians stated, that forced them to act.

9. For details on how the truce between the two sides was worked out, see Johnson, "Burkina-Mali War, pp. 294–308.

10. See "Border Conflict at the Hague," *West Africa*, June 30, 1986, p. 1393.

11. The International Court of Justice's decision was Solomonic: The contested territory was divided in half, with Mali given the western portion, containing four villages that it had consistently claimed were Malian. Radio Mali characterized the decision in conciliatory language: "The Burkinabe and Malian people have just won a joint and brilliant historical victory." See "Mali: Verdict on Burkina Dispute," *West Africa*, January 5, 1987, p. 37.

12. For details on Mali's early diplomatic relations in Africa, see Decraene, *Le Mali*, pp. 77–80.

13. See: "CEAO: Survival and Change," March 31, 1986, p. 655, and "Scandal Clouds West African Summit," *Africa Report*, January/February 1985, p. 38.

14. For details on Mali's early East-West relations, see Decraene, *Le Mali*, pp. 76–77, and Gerard Brasseur, *Le Mali*, Paris, La Documentation Française, 1974, pp. 24–25.

15. Formal invitations to Malian officials to attend functions at the residence of the U.S. ambassador were frequently ignored. The homes of most Americans were under surveillance, and Malians seen visiting them were sometimes threatened by the security services with job loss and imprisonment. Most Malians, except those who worked there, were fearful of entering the U.S. embassy in Bamako.

16. Personal communications from U.S. diplomats at the U.S. embassy, Bamako, and at the Department of State, 1970s and 1980s.

17. See Gerald M. Boyd, "Bush Announces Plan to Aid 'Free Market' Farming in Mali," *New York Times*, March 10, 1985.

18. President Traoré was also given an official luncheon at the U.S. Department of State on October 6, 1988, at which Maureen Reagan, the president's daughter, was in attendance. He met with the Congressional leaders, Afro-American businessmen, and received an honorary doctorate degree from Central State University at Wilberforce, Ohio, where he gave a speech on human rights.

Selected Bibliography

Introduction

Brasseur, Gerard. *Le Mali*. Paris, La Documentation Française, 1974.

Decraene, Philippe. *Le Mali*. Presses Universitaires de France, 1980.

Delafosse, Maurice. *Haut-Sénégal Niger*. Paris, Larose, 1912, 3 vols., reprinted, Paris, Maisonneuve et Larose, 1972, 3 vols.

Imperato, Pascal James. *Historical Dictionary of Mali*, 2nd ed. Metuchen, N.J. and London, Scarecrow Press, 1986.

Imperato, Pascal James, and Imperato, Eleanor M. *Mali: A Handbook of Historical Statistics*. Boston, G. K. Hall, 1982.

Jouve, Edmond. *La République du Mali*. Paris, Berger-Levrault, 1974.

Kamian, Bakari. *Connaissance de la République du Mali*. Bamako, Secrétariat d'Etat à l'information et au Tourisme, 1962.

Mali, Encyclopédie Africaine et Malagache. Paris, Librairie Larousse, 1964.

Meggle, Armand. *Terres Françaises: Afrique Occidentale Française*, vol. 14. Paris, Société Française d'Editions, 1931.

N'Diaye, Bokar. *Groupes ethniques au Mali*. Bamako, Editions Populaires, 1970.

Early History

Abitol, Michel. *Tombouctou et les Arma*. Paris, Maisonneuve et Larose, 1979.

Ba, Amadou Hampaté, and Daget, Jacques. *L'Empire Peul du Macina*, vol. 1, 1818–1853. Paris, Mouton, 1962.

Bovill, E. W. *The Golden Trade of the Moors*. London, Oxford University Press, 1958.

Dunn, Ross E. *The Adventures of Ibn Battuta. A Muslim Traveler of the Fourteenth Century*. Berkeley, University of California Press, 1987.

Imperato, Pascal James. *Historical Dictionary of Mali*, 2nd ed. Metuchen, N.J., and London, Scarecrow Press, 1986.

McIntosh, Susan K., and McIntosh, Roderick J. "Finding West Africa's Oldest City," *National Geographic* 162:396–418, 1982.

Monteil, Charles. *Une Cité soudanaise, Djénné, métropole du delta central du Niger,* Paris, Société d'Editions Géographiques, Maritime et Coloniales, 1932, 2nd ed. London, International African Institute, 1971.

Oloruntimehin, B. O. *The Segu Tukulor Empire.* London, Longmans, 1972.

Roberts, Richard. *Warriors, Slaves and Merchants: The State and the Economy in the Middle Niger Valley 1700–1914.* Stanford, Stanford University Press, 1987.

Robinson, David. *The Holy War of Umar Tal: The Western Sudan in the Mid-Nineteenth Century.* Oxford, Oxford University Press, 1985.

Saad, Elias N. *Social History of Timbuctoo.* Cambridge, Cambridge University Press, 1983.

Tauxier, Louis. *Histoire des Bambara.* Paris, Librairie Orientaliste Paul Geuthner, 1942.

Conquest, Colonial Rule, and Independence

Balesi, Charles John. *From Adversaries to Comrade-in-Arms: West Africans and the French Military, 1885–1918.* Waltham, Mass., Crossroads Press, 1979.

Barth, Heinrich. *Travels and Discoveries in North and Central Africa,* centenary ed. 1865–1965. London, Frank Cass, 1965.

Caillié, Réné. *Travels Through Central Africa to Timbuctoo,* vols. 1 and 2. London, Frank Cass, 1968.

Foltz, William J. *From French West Africa to the Mali Federation.* New Haven and London, Yale University Press, 1965.

Gardner, Brian. *The Quest for Timbuctoo.* New York, Harcourt, Brace and World, 1968.

Kanya-Forstner, A. S. *The Conquest of the Western Sudan: A Study in French Military Imperialism.* Cambridge, Cambridge University Press, 1969.

Méniaud, Jacques. *Les Pionniers du Soudan avant, avec et après Archinard (1879–1894),* 2 vols. Paris, Société des Publications Modernes, 1931.

Roberts, S. H. *History of French Colonial Policy (1870–1925),* 2 vols. London, King, 1929.

Snyder, Frank G. *One-Party Government in Mali: Transition Toward Control.* New Haven and London, Yale University Press, 1965.

Thompson, Virginia, and Adloff, Richard. *French West Africa.* Stanford, Stanford University Press, 1958.

Malian Politics Since Independence

An I de la révolution, 1967. Bamako, Imprimerie Nationale, 1968.

Bennett, Valerie Pleve. "Military Government in Mali," *Journal of Modern African Studies* 13:249–266, 1975.

Diarrah, Cheick Oumar. *Le Mali de Modibo Keita,* Paris, Editions l'Harmattan, 1986.

Golan, Tamar. "Anatomie du coup d'état malien du 19 Novembre, 1968," *Révue française d'Etudes politiques africaines* 99:27–51, 1974.

———. "The Yoro Diakite Affair," *West Africa,* August 20, 1973, pp. 1147–1149.

Hazard, John N. "Mali's Socialism and the Soviet Legal Model," *Yale Law Journal* 77:28–69, 1967.

Pierot, Robert. *L'administration Malienne*. Paris, Berger-Levrault, 1979.

Rawson, David P. "Mali: Soldiers as Politicians," in *The Performance of Soldiers as Governors: African Politics and the African Military*, ed. Isaac James Mowoe. Washington, D.C., University Press of America, 1980.

Schissel, Howard. "Mali: No More Room for Maneuver," *Africa Report* 20:63–66, 1964.

Snyder, Francis Gregory. "The Keita Decade, 1. An Era Ends in Mali," *Africa Report* 14:16–22, 1969.

———. "The Political Thought of Modibo Keita," *Journal of Modern African Studies* 5:79–106, 1967.

Wolpin, Miles D. "Dependency and Conservative Militarism in Mali," *Journal of Modern African Studies* 13:585–620, 1975.

Culture and Society

Brenner, Louis. *West African Sufi: The Religious Heritage and Spiritual Search of Cerno Bokar Saalif Taal*. Berkeley, University of California Press, 1984.

Dieterlen, Germaine. *Essai sur la religion Bambara*. Paris, Presses Universitaires de France, 1951.

Ezra, Kate. *Art of the Dogon: Selections from the Lester Wunderman Collection*. New York, Metropolitan Museum of Art/Harry N. Abrams, 1988.

Griaule, Marcel. *Masques Dogons*. Paris, Institut d'Ethnologie, 1963.

Griaule, Marcel, and Dieterlen, Germaine. *Le renard pâle*. Paris, Institut d'Ethnologie, 1965.

Imperato, Pascal James. "Blankets and Covers from the Niger Bend," *African Arts* 12:38–43, 1979.

———. *Buffoons, Queens and Wooden Horsemen: The Dyo and Gouan Societies of the Bambara of Mali*. Manhasset, N.Y., Kilima House Publishers, 1983.

———. "The Dance of the Tyi Wara," *African Arts* 4:8–13, 71–80, 1970.

———. *Dogon Cliff Dwellers: The Art of Mali's Mountain People*. L. Kahan Gallery/African Arts, 1978.

———. "Africa—Health," *Encyclopedia Americana*, International Edition. Danbury, Conn., Grolier, 1988, pp. 282–284.

Kaba, Lansiné. *The Wahhabiyya: Islamic Reform and Politics in French West Africa*. Evanston, Ill., Northwestern University Press, 1974.

McNaughton, Patrick R. *Iron Art of the Blacksmith in the Western Sudan*. West Lafayette, Ind., Purdue University Press, 1975.

———. *The Mande Blacksmiths. Knowledge, Power, and Art in West Africa*. Bloomington and Indianapolis, Indiana University Press, 1988.

Paques, Viviana. *Les Bambara*. Paris, Presses Universitaires de France, 1974.

Plan décennal (1 juillet 1966–30 juin 1976) de développement des services de santé. Bamako, Ministère de la Santé Publique et des Affaires Sociales, 1966.

Zahan, Dominique. *Antilopes du Soleil: Arts et Rites Agraires d'Afrique Noir*. Vienna, A. Schendl, 1980.

———. *The Bambara*. Leiden, E. J. Brill, 1974.

The Economy

Amin, Samir. *Trois expériences africaines de développement: Le Mali, la Guinée, le Ghana*. Paris, Presses Universitaires de France.

Bélimé, Emile. *Les Travaux du Niger*. Lille, Martin-Mamy, 1940.

Biarnes, Pierre. "Mali—A Bottomless Pit for Investors," *Economist*, May 9, 1981.

Crum, David. "Mali and the U.M.O.A.: A Case Study of Economic Integration," *Journal of Modern African Studies* 22:469–486, 1984.

Ernst, Klaus. *Tradition and Progress in the African Village: Non-Capitalist Transformation of Rural Communities in Mali*, trans. Salomea Genin, Jurgen Herzog. New York, St. Martin's Press, 1976.

Glantz, Michael H. (ed.). *The Politics of Natural Disaster: The Case of the Sahel Drought*. New York, Praeger, 1976.

Jones, William I. "The Keita Decade. 2. Economics of the Coup," *Africa Report* 14, 3/4:23–26, 51–53, 1969.

Keita, Rokiatou N'Diaye. *Kayes et le Haut Sénégal*, vol. 1, *Les étapes de la croissance urbaine*, vol. 2, *La Ville de Kayes*. Bamako, Editions Populaires, 1972.

Lewis, John Van Dusen. "Small Farmer Credit and the Village Production Unit in Rural Mali," *African Studies Review* 21, 3:29–48, 1978.

Magasa, Amidu, *Papa-commandant a jété·un grand filet devant nous, les exploités des rives Niger (1902–1962)*. Paris, Maspero, 1978.

Somerville, Carolyn M. *Drought and AID in the Sahel*. Boulder and London, Westview Press, 1986.

Stryker, Derik J. "The Malian Cattle Industry: Opportunity and Dilemma," *Journal of Modern African Studies* 12:3–11, 1974.

Szabo, André. *Améliorations Possibles de l'Utilisation des Produits de la Pêche*. Rome, United Nations Food and Agriculture Organization, 1970.

———. "Preventing Post-Harvest Losses of Dried Fish: A Proposal," *Kidima: Israel Journal of Development* 7, 2:17–20, 1982.

Mali's International Relations

Brasseur, Gerard. *Le Mali*. Paris, La Documentation Française, 1974.

Johnson, Segun. "Burkina-Mali War: Is Nigeria Still a Regional Power," *India Quarterly*, July-September, 1986, pp. 294–308.

Mortimer, Edward. *France and the Africans, 1944–1960: A Political History*. New York, Walker, 1969.

Thiam, Doudou. *The Foreign Policy of African States*. New York, Praeger, 1965.

Acronyms

AIDS	Acquired Immunodeficiency Syndrome
AMPA	Agence Malienne de Presse et de Publicité
ANAD	West African Non-Aggression and Defense Accord
ARP	Amis du Rassemblement Populaire du Soudan Français
BCEAO	Banque Centrale des Etats d'Afrique de l'Ouest
BEC	Bureau Executif Central
CCSE	Commission des Comités Syndicaux des Enseignants
CEAO	Communauté Economique de l'Afrique de l'Ouest
CFA	Communauté Financière Africaine
CILSS	Comité Permanent Inter-Etats de Lutte Contre la Secheresse dans le Sahel
CMLN	Comité Militaire de Liberation Nationale
CNDR	Comité National de Défense de la Révolution
DEF	Diplôme des Etudes Fondamentales
ECOWAS	Economic Community of West African States
FAO	Food and Agriculture Organization
GEC	Groupes d'Etudes Communistes
GDP	Gross Domestic Product
HIV	Human Immunodeficiency Virus
IMF	International Monetary Fund
OAU	Organization of African Unity
OCAM	Organisation Commune Africaine at Malagache
OCCGE	Organisation de Coordination et de Coopération pour la Lutte contre les Grandes Endémies
OERS	Organisation des Etats Riverains du Sénégal
OMVS	Organisation pour la Mise-en-Valeur du Fleuve Sénégal
OPAM	Office des Produits Agricoles du Mali
OPEC	Organization of Petroleum Exporting Countries
PDS	Parti Démocratique Soudanais
PLO	Palestine Liberation Organization
POLISARIO	Front Populaire pour la Libération de la Saguiat et Hamra et du Rio de Oro

163

PPS   Parti Progressiste Soudanais
PRC   People's Republic of China
RDA   Rassemblement Démocratique Africain
SCINFOMA   Service Cinématographique du Ministère de l'Information du Mali
SCOA   Société Commerciale de l'Ouest Africain
SNEC   Syndicat National de l'Education et de la Culture
SOMIEX   Société Malienne d'Importation et d'Exportation
UDPM   Union Démocratique du Peuple Malien
UN   United Nations
UNEEM   Union Nationale des Etudiants et des Elèves du Mali
UNFM   Union Nationale des Femmes Maliennes
UNTM   Union Nationale des Travailleurs du Mali
US   Union Soudanaise
USAID   U.S. Agency for International Development
US-RDA   Union Soudanaise–Rassemblement Démocratique Africain
WHO   World Health Organization

Index

165